SD-84

Columbia University

Contributions to Education

Teachers College Series

No. 618

AMS PRESS
NEW YORK

CENTRALIZING TENDENCIES IN THE ADMINISTRATION OF PUBLIC EDUCATION

A STUDY OF LEGISLATION FOR SCHOOLS IN NORTH CAROLINA, MARYLAND, AND NEW YORK SINCE 1900

By GEORGE D. STRAYER, JR., PH.D.

TEACHERS COLLEGE, COLUMBIA UNIVERSITY
CONTRIBUTIONS TO EDUCATION, NO. 618

Published with the Approval of
Professor JOHN K. NORTON, *Sponsor*

BUREAU OF PUBLICATIONS
Teachers College, Columbia University
NEW YORK CITY
1934

Library of Congress Cataloging in Publication Data

Strayer, George Drayton, 1906-
    Centralizing tendencies in the administration of
public education.

    Reprint of the 1934 ed., issued in series: Teachers
College, Columbia University. Contributions to educa-
tion, no. 618.
    Originally presented as the author's thesis, Columbia.
    Bibliography: p.
    1. School management and organization--Atlantic
States. 2. Education and state--United States.
3. Educational law and legislation--Atlantic States.
I. Title. II. Series: Columbia University.
Teachers College. Contributions to education, no. 618.
LB2806.S7 1972   379'.1535   74-177739
ISBN 0-404-55618-3

Reprinted by Special Arrangement with Teachers
College Press, New York, New York

From the edition of 1934, New York
First AMS edition published in 1972
Manufactured in the United States

AMS PRESS, INC.
NEW YORK, N. Y.   10003

ACKNOWLEDGMENTS

THE writer wishes to express his appreciation for the guidance and advice of his sponsor, Professor John K. Norton, and the helpful criticisms and suggestions contributed by Professor Isaac L. Kandel and Professor Edward H. Reisner of his dissertation committee. He is indebted to Mr. Miles O. Price, Law Librarian of Columbia University, for his courtesy and coöperation in making available the facilities of the Law Library of Columbia University. The study was suggested by the writer's father, Professor George D. Strayer, for whose stimulation and encouragement he is deeply grateful.

G. D. S., JR.

CONTENTS

CONTENTS

CENTRALIZING TENDENCIES IN THE ADMINISTRATION OF PUBLIC EDUCATION

CHAPTER I

THE PROBLEM OF CENTRALIZATION IN THE ADMINISTRATION OF EDUCATION

STUDENTS of comparative education have remarked that the type of educational administration to be found in any country is determined not simply by the theory of education which is prevalent but also by the theory of government which prevails. As Kandel[1] points out, a country having an authoritarian government usually develops a highly centralized system of educational administration, while a country having a federative type of government usually allows a considerable degree of freedom to local areas and exercises a minimum of administrative authority over them.

Centralized systems of educational administration tend to control the schools through the authority of the state; decentralized systems are prone to exercise leadership and guidance in stimulating local authorities to provide adequate educational facilities. Education has a definite place in the state and in the social order as one of the universal services by means of which the state develops its social and economic resources. According to MacIver,

It is surely significant that here [in education] the state has taken over and vastly developed a task which was formerly assigned to the family and then extended by special associations such as the guild and the church. Of course, the family still acts as an agency of education, and always must, but it is unqualified to give its members the continuous training requisite for life in a civilized community. It is the state which inevitably took over this function. It could do so just because (unlike the church) it has no particularist interest, because therefore it can call on every one to assist in a service and undertake obligations whose universal character is clear, because also it alone can command the resources for the greatest of those enterprises which return their "dividend" invisibly and to the whole community. What applies to education applies also, and for the same reasons, to the general promotion of the cultural life. Whatever can be done in this direction—and it leads into a great field of

[1] For a full treatment of this topic, see Chapter V, "Administration of Education," in *Comparative Education* by I. L. Kandel.

1

unexplored possibilities—without taking sides in the cultural issues on which men are seriously divided, and without infringing the liberty which is the source of achievement, the state can, and indeed ought to do.[2]

The purpose of educational administration is well expressed by Kandel in the following words:

Fundamentally the purpose of educational administration is to bring pupils and teachers together under such conditions as will most successfully promote the ends of education. . . .[3]

Public schools in a democracy must serve all groups equally, and, as has been suggested above, are affected by the theory of government and the theory of education which prevail in the society from which they derive their support.

The federative form of government existing in the United States seems to suggest a decentralized type of administration, allowing the areas within the states considerable degree of freedom and initiative as well as permitting opportunity for state rather than national control of education.

One of the most important issues with which thoughtful school administrators in the United States are concerned is this problem of centralization and the forces working for and against it. The major aspect of the problem is the relationship of the state to the localities within its borders in matters concerning the provision of education. Holcombe discusses this relationship as follows:

There is no common rule for the division of power between the different central educational authorities, and, in general, no systematic arrangements for effective coöperation between them.

It is apparent that there is a real need for reorganization and consolidation in the field of state educational administration. As yet, however, little has been accomplished towards meeting this need. Partly because the office of state superintendent of public instruction is generally made elective by the constitution and partly for other reasons, the reorganization movement has left the central educational agencies substantially unchanged.[4]

In the early development of education in the United States, the locality rather than the state or the nation exercised the chief authority. The administration of public education began in the towns, the district, and the township. During the nineteenth century, as expenditures and the provision of educational opportunities continued to increase, it became evident that small local

---

[2] MacIver, R. M., *The Modern State*, pp. 187–88.   [3] Kandel, I. L., *op. cit.*, p. 211.
[4] Holcombe, Arthur N., *State Government in the United States*, pp. 381–82.

units of administration were inefficient and costly.[5] The transfer of powers and responsibilities from smaller to larger units of administration was frequently contemporaneous with increased state support for the public schools. Whether or not a causal relationship existed between these two movements was as controversial an issue in the latter part of the nineteenth century as it is today.

A dissertation written in 1898 by Webster held that state aid "naturally and necessarily led" to state control.[6] Fairlie, whose dissertation was published in the same year, suggested that central "control" had been "closely connected with the increase of state grants," but that state aid did not "seem to have been given for the purpose of establishing control."[7] He further declared that state appropriations had rendered necessary state supervision and that the increase of state grants had made the "control" of local authorities more complete and effective.[8] The following paragraph indicates that Fairlie considered that this "control" would not interfere with the exercise of local initiative by the school districts throughout the state:

> It should, however, be noticed that the system of state supervision in no way restricts the local authorities in adding to their educational arrangements. It is a control exercised to bring the schools throughout the state up to a minimum standard; beyond that, the local officials are free to extend their school system to any degree.[9]

There has been a general trend throughout our educational history, and more markedly so in recent decades, toward an increase in the educational activities of the state government; that is, a tendency toward centralization of various educational functions and services in that governmental unit. In consequence, at the present time the various states present situations in which education, although still essentially locally administered, is controlled in many important aspects by the central rather than the

---

[5] "The evils of the district system and the impossibility of ever equalizing school revenues, educational opportunities, and school burdens, as long as the district or any other similar small unit is maintained as the controlling source of school revenue, have been pointed out by every leading authority on the organization and support of public schools for the last hundred years. These leaders have been unanimous in their condemnation of the district system and in their support of a larger school unit."—Swift, Fletcher Harper, *Federal and State Policies in Public School Finance in the United States*, p. 103.

[6] Webster, William C., *Recent Centralizing Tendencies in State Educational Administration*, p. 13.   [7] Fairlie, John A., *The Centralization of Administration in New York State*, p. 33.
[8] *Ibid.*, p. 33.   [9] *Ibid.*, p. 57.

local units of educational government.[10]   For the purpose of this study, centralization is defined as the transfer by law of control or authority from a local administrative unit to the state.

In his book on state school administration, Cubberley comments on the fact that

. . . local governing authorities act as agents for the state and can do only those things which the school law permits of being done.

Powers not enumerated in the law are usually held by the courts as not existing; schools not conducted in conformity with the state school law may have state aid withheld; and local failure to comply with the mandates of the school law may result in court action to compel compliance, or even in the state school authorities stepping in and assuming control of the schools that the educational rights of the children of the community may be protected.[11]

The ability of the state to enforce the laws applying to education is dependent upon the adequacy of the staff provided in the state education office.   While the median size of staff of State Departments of Education increased from three in 1900 to twenty-eight in 1930,[12] there were still seven states having fewer than fifteen staff members and six states having no State Board of Education in 1930.[13]   The power and prestige of the State Department of Education is also somewhat dependent upon the method of selecting the chief state school officer.   The method of selection has changed but little since 1890.   In that year in twenty-nine states the chief state school officer was elected by popular vote, while in fifteen (including two territories) the official was appointed by the Governor, the State Board of Education, the Legislature, or the Supreme Court.   Two states had no chief state school officer, and two states were still unorganized territory. In 1930 thirty-three chief state school officers were elected by popular vote and seventeen were appointed by the Governor or by the State Board of Education.[14]

[10] See discussions of centralization in *Recent Social Trends in the United States*, Vol. II, Chap. XXV, "The Growth of Governmental Functions," by Carroll H. Wooddy, p. 1294; Chap. XXVII, "Public Administration," by Leonard D. White, pp. 1397–99.

[11] Cubberley, Ellwood P., *State School Administration*, p. 126.

[12] National Education Association, Research Division, *Studies in State Educational Administration*, No. 9, p. 6, March, 1931.

[13] State Education Departments, on the whole, have not been adequately staffed to provide more than routine services to the school districts of the states.   See *Recent Social Trends, op. cit.*, Chap. XXV, p. 1302.

[14] "Idaho and Wyoming have two state school officials, one elected by popular vote and the other appointed by the State Board of Education.   Both are included here."—National Education Association, Research Division, *op. cit.*, p. 31.

Although uniform educational opportunities do not exist throughout any one of the forty-eight states and few of the State Departments of Education are strong enough to direct a centralized program of public education, many changes have taken place since the beginning of the century pointing toward a more unified system of educational offerings and a more centralized method of educational administration.[15]

In 1898 Webster called attention to the decline of the "district system" and the increase in state control over many branches of school administration, especially in regard to textbooks, courses of study, certification of teachers, compulsory attendance, and the length of the school term. He stated that

. . . the establishment of state school funds, then, became the basis of a distinctive state policy, and inaugurated a system of state control and intervention in the field of education.[16]

It is of interest in this connection to note another statement by the same author to the effect that "the principle of state aid to common school education is firmly established."[17]

The establishment of state school funds, state systems of taxation for public schools, and larger local units of administration, and the acceptance of the principle of state aid were certainly among the pioneer factors which contributed to tendencies toward the furtherance of centralization of educational administration.

It is significant that the assumption of new powers by the states (through new legislation, court interpretation of existing legislation, or new rules and regulations) was considered an "intervention" in the realm of local control, and the beginnings of state aid were thought "naturally and necessarily" to lead to state control.

One of the forces which contributed to the local control of education was the American belief in liberty and the rights of the individual. The ideal of equality of opportunity is closely associated with this belief in freedom and in individual rights. This democratic ideal has been expressed perhaps more clearly in relationship to public education than in any other activity of American life.

---

[15] "The evidence of the last thirty years demonstrates a steady accretion of power and influence by the state governments over the administrative operations of local officials especially in the fields of public finance, education, health, and highways. . . ."—*Recent Social Trends, op. cit.,* Chap. XXVII, p. 1394.　[16] Webster, William C., *op. cit.,* p. 14.　[17] *Ibid.,* p. 12.

The early recognition in the United States of the relationship of education to the ideal of democracy was a strong drive toward local control of schools. This relationship is expressed by Bryce as follows:

Modern democratic theory rests on two doctrines as its two sustaining pillars: that the gift of the suffrage creates the will to use it, and that the gift of knowledge creates the capacity to use the suffrage aright. From this it is commonly assumed to follow that the more educated a democracy is, the better will its government be. This view, being hopeful, was and is popular. It derived strength from the fact that all the despotic governments of sixty years ago, and some of them down to our own day, were either indifferent or hostile to the spread of education among their subjects, because they feared that knowledge and intelligence would create a wish for freedom, and remembered that such old movements of revolt as Wat Tyler's rising in 1381 and the Peasants' War in Germany in 1522, had failed largely because the discontented subjects did not know how to combine.[18]

Democracy was understood to mean not only universal participation of all men in the formation of policies but also opportunity for everyone to take part in their administration. There was no area of government where this idea was more certainly accepted than in the support and control of schools.

Another force which was of great importance in the development of local control of schools was the self-reliance demanded of the individual and of the community in which he lived, by the isolated conditions of frontier life. Both transportation and communication were slow and unreliable.[19] There were few national newspapers or magazines. The people of each locality were under the necessity of developing locally whatever provisions for education their children were to enjoy.

The foregoing are some of the forces which operated to bring about in the United States a decentralized system of public schools, in which the determination of the purposes of education, its organization, administration, and control, have tended to be centered in the individual community rather than in the state or the nation.[20]

A variety of conditions have operated, with increasing effect in

[18] Bryce, James, *Modern Democracies*, Vol. I, p. 70.

[19] "Broadly speaking, the drive toward centralization is animated by the desire for better service or more effective regulation, and is made possible by the great technical improvements in the art of communication and transportation."—White, Leonard D., *Trends in Public Administration*, p. 18.

[20] For other causes of the development of the school as a local institution see *Public School Administration* by Ellwood P. Cubberley, Chap. I–III.

recent decades, to make imperative an adjustment of the relationship between the various levels of government and the conduct of education. For example, the change from a rather simple and self-contained economic system, in which wealth was relatively evenly distributed and existed largely in the form of property, to an extremely complex, interdependent economic order in which taxpaying ability resides in a variety of complicated forms, and the fact that wealth, originating from nation-wide if not world-wide economic activity, tends to concentrate in small areas, have made increasing numbers of local schools impotent in attempting to provide adequate provision for education. According to Holcombe,

The case for a larger measure of centralization than heretofore has been unanswerable. It rests partly upon the advance of science, which has increased the demands of the people upon their governments, and partly upon the mere growth of population, which compels governments to be more active. The public business has become more extensive than formerly, more costly, and more exacting in the technical requirements it imposes upon public officers. Small and weak administrative areas can not supply the necessary technicians or can not afford to employ them, and find local politicians or amateur administrators an increasingly unsatisfactory substitute for experts. State governments can organize their own services, when local administrative systems fail, but strictly local services are dependent upon suitable local administrative areas and services of more general utility are not easily released from the bondage of local government systems. Administrative areas which were created to meet the needs of earlier times, become less and less suitable under the changing circumstances of the present day. Larger areas become increasingly desirable, both because in urban districts the population tends to grow ever larger and to occupy larger areas, and because in rural districts larger populations are needed to support modern public services and only larger areas can supply such populations.[21]

These conditions are making necessary substantial modifications of the traditional division of responsibility between the forty-eight state governments and the local units of school administration within their borders. What is the nature of these adjustments? Are they taking place as a result of carefully thought-out principles of administration, or a philosophy of the appropriate relationship of the state and local units of government, or are they taking place as a result of opportunistic and chance factors and forces?

It is the purpose of this study to shed some light on the fore-

[21] Holcombe, Arthur N., *op. cit.*, pp. 608-09.

going questions.   It will examine in detail the trends of the more important legislation affecting the relationship of the state government to education in each of three states, and will consider these trends in the light of certain criteria or principles which are believed to be valuable in determining their significance for educational development.

Legally the control of education is a state function, but in practice, owing to factors such as those already described, the actual amount of control exercised by the state has been small. The result has been to give certain distinctive characteristics to American education, some of which have added to its effectiveness and vitality.   This policy has also resulted in certain weaknesses in the American schools which need to be examined carefully.   In this situation American education is confronted with the problem of preserving those factors of local participation which contribute, and which may be expected to continue to contribute, to educational efficiency, while at the same time transferring to state authority certain duties affecting the maintenance of schools which changed circumstances no longer permit the locality to perform.

This study, in attempting to illuminate this crucial and difficult field, will present a detailed analysis of the changes in the relationship of the state to the local administrative area which have been determined by legislation since 1900.   The analysis will be based on an intensive study of educational legislation in three states, as well as on a study of certain secondary source material.

The states chosen for study are North Carolina, Maryland, and New York.   Their choice is based on the following considerations:

1. It is necessary, for practical reasons, to limit the study.

2. It is known that in these three states considerable centralization has occurred.   They have traveled a long way in the direction of an adjustment of state and local relationships. It is not contended that these states are necessarily the ones which have gone farthest in this respect or that the adjustments they have made are typical for the other forty-five states.

In considering the facts which will be revealed concerning the trends of educational legislation in these states, it is desirable to bear in mind certain standards of judgment with respect to the significance of these trends. This will permit their logical appraisal and a better estimation of their significance.

It is not claimed that these criteria or principles are the only ones which might be used, that they are all-inclusive, or that they are necessarily the final word on the standards which should govern the relationship of the state and the localities in the provision of educational facilities. It is believed, however, that they are of considerable importance and that their application to the facts revealed concerning legislation for education in the three states studied will aid in understanding the significance of these legislative changes.

THE CRITERIA

I. *Equalization of educational opportunity and support should be provided.*

This criterion is fundamental. It is based on the belief that all children should be guaranteed an educational opportunity up to a prescribed minimum, or the very purpose of public education is thwarted. Any relationship between the state and its localities that does not offer a reasonable guarantee of provision for the education of every child within the localities is inefficient for the purpose of public education and is a denial of the commonly accepted principle that education is a function of the state. Government exists not to carry out certain abstract principles of the relationship of one governmental level to another but to promote social progress—in the case at hand, the reasonably effective education of all the children within the state. Any arrangement which does not guarantee provisions whereby this end may be accomplished is, therefore, indefensible.

Equity and justice require that the cost of these minimum educational facilities shall rest with equal burden upon the economic resources of the state. This requisite is supported by the accepted principles of taxation and by the principle of equity which urges that services essential to the common welfare be paid for by a method which places an equal burden upon all the people in whose interest these services are maintained. These essentials were clearly defined in 1925 by the Educational Finance Inquiry in these words:

To carry into effect the principle of "equalization of educational opportunity" and "equalization of school support" as commonly understood, it would be necessary (1) to establish schools or make other arrangements sufficient to furnish the children in every locality within the state with equal educational opportunities up to some prescribed minimum; (2) to raise the funds necessary for this purpose by local or state taxation adjusted in such manner as to bear upon the people in all localities at the same rate in relation to their taxpaying ability; and (3) to provide adequately either for the supervision and control of all the schools, or for their direct administration, by a state department of education.[22]

This principle has found repeated acceptance since it was first stated by the Educational Finance Inquiry Commission. The report of the National Conference on the Financing of Education, held under the auspices of the Joint Commission on the Emergency in Education of the National Education Association and the Department of Superintendence in 1933, proposed the following plan as "the basic principle of state support":

The experience of the past decade supports the adoption of the principle of the equalization of educational opportunity in future state support programs. *This principle calls upon the state to equalize educational opportunity and the burden of its support up to a reasonably satisfactory minimum.* It involves an equality and reasonableness of burden among local units towards the support of a determined educational program. The state provides that portion of the support of the minimum program beyond the locality's contribution. Below the minimum educational program no community should be allowed to drop in school opportunity, but above it any local unit should be permitted to go upon its own initiative and own extra support. Such a principle in the field of school finance provides a children's charter and at the same time it promotes tax equity.[23]

A similar statement of the same principle is contained in a report made in 1933 by the Governor's Committee on the Costs of Public Education in the State of New York:

We must continue to offer equal opportunity to the children of New York. This means that every effort must be made to continue the principle of providing that the burden fall equally upon all parts of the state, and that administrative practices, methods of teaching, and subjects taught should be adjusted to the needs of all classes, groups, and types of children. We must remember that equality of opportunity is not identity of opportunity, and that people who differ are not likely to receive equal consideration if they are all treated in the same way.[24]

[22] The Educational Finance Inquiry Commission, *Educational Finance Inquiry*, Vol. I (by George D. Strayer and Robert M. Haig), *The Financing of Education in the State of New York,* p. 174.
[23] Joint Commission on the Emergency in Education, *Report of National Conference on the Financing of Education*, p. 23.
[24] Governor's Committee on the Costs of Public Education in the State of New York, *Report,* p. 14.

In the light of these and other statements of this principle by students of the problem of support, it is held that the first criterion —*equalization of educational opportunity and support should be provided*—is justified for use in this study.

II. *Certain areas of local participation should be preserved in order that adaptation of the educational program may be guaranteed and efficiency maintained. Centralization should be confined to those phases of education classified as "externa," leaving matters classified as "interna" to be regulated by local school districts.*[25]

A consideration of the principle of equalization of educational opportunity and support, in relation to its practical application, brings up many questions. Will the provision of equal educational opportunity in all parts of the state tend to destroy initiative in the local units, to limit experimentation, or to weaken the feeling of responsibility in the different localities? Russell finds in the European practice of dividing school administration into "interna" and "externa" a contribution toward the solution of these problems.

In Europe there is a division of school administration that is so universally understood and so generally accepted that one fails to find a definition or explanation. It is accepted as if no other attitude were ever considered. In the law, in official handbooks, in textbooks we find reference to the "interna" and the "externa"; internal and external administration of schools. Internal has to do with what is taught, how it is taught, how the teacher is trained, and the life and spirit of the school. External deals with seeing that the pupils attend, providing suitable places for instruction, keeping the school building clean and habitable, the pupils well, the teachers paid, the equipment provided. The chalk that the teacher uses is external; what he writes with the chalk, internal. His salary is external; what he teaches and the way he does it, internal. That the pupil shall be given glasses so that he may read is external; what he reads is internal. The pupils march out of the building to study plants in the garden; this is internal. The janitor walks into the building to fire the stove; this is external. The material side of education is external; the spiritual and mental side is internal. So commonly is this concept accepted in Europe that different school officials are assigned; and in general the external is controlled and supported by governmental units different from those controlling and supporting the internal. . . .

This division of school administration points the way, as I see it, to the solution of the American problem. We need centralization to provide equality; we fear centralization as a menace to our liberty. Very well! Let us agree to

---

[25] Making allowance for the legitimate exercise of leadership on the part of the state education authorities in all that affects the quality of instruction in the schools.

centralize the externals, reserving to the localities complete control over the internals.[26]

Laski, who favors decentralization wherever possible, makes an exception in the case of education. He argues that

It is, for example, legitimate to allow a town to decide whether or not it desires municipal electricity; it is illegitimate to allow it to decide whether it desires an educational system. In services, that is to say, of which the incidence of interest is almost entirely local, the right of the central government to intervene is the better exercised the less it exists.[27]

Kandel, on the other hand, sees a danger in centralizing certain aspects of the administration of education, and points out the need of increased participation of the public:

In the last analysis the progress of education depends upon public enlightenment and willingness to support it. This means, not merely the education of the public through parents' organizations and other methods of propaganda, but measures for increased participation of the public in the administration of education. . . . Centralized systems of education may achieve standards of excellence which are sometimes not attained in systems administered locally, but they neither create nor are they susceptible to changing public demands. Education is a living thing and cannot, without seeming to be artificial, be created according to one pattern applicable over an extensive area.[28]

Any arbitrary rule or law of a State Department of Education or a State Board of Education which denies opportunity for participation or interpretation by the locality essentially works against local initiative and opportunity for experimentation. The right of appeal from decisions of a State Department or State Board of Education might prevent, of course, the possibility of any absolute "dictatorship."

There are many centralizing tendencies which permit local initiative and experimentation to continue undisturbed; there are others which detract slightly from local power; while, of course, certain of them leave little power or responsibility with the locality. The second criterion cannot be applied indiscriminately, for there are some parts of the educational program which manifestly are better served under the control of the central authority than under the local unit of authority.

A plea for local government by Laski indicates a few of the advantages:

[26] Russell, William F., "School Administration and Conflicting American Ideals." *Teachers College Record*, Vol. XXXI, No. 1, pp. 21–23, October, 1929.
[27] Laski, Harold J., *A Grammar of Politics*, p. 61.   [28] Kandel, I. L., *op. cit.*, p. 683

Local governmeht, in other words, is educative in perhaps a higher degree, at least contingently, than any other part of government. And it must be remembered that there is no other way of bringing the mass of citizens into intimate contact with the persons responsible for decisions. It is clear that any great degree of centralization must mean, and can only mean, a bureaucratic system. No legislative assembly in the world will be able, however greedy of power, to make decisions upon more than the largest outlines of local problems. The application of their details will be left to the departments. Appointed officials will therefore dominate them, and they will never be genuinely accessible to public opinion.[29]

The recognition of the importance of the local influence does not mean, however, that everything should be controlled by the local authority. In fact, if this were the case, education under the present changed conditions would suffer, if not disappear, in many local communities. What, then, are the areas of local participation which are essential to adequacy and efficiency? What are some of the areas which may properly be assumed by the state?

Kandel, in his *Essays in Comparative Education*, discusses the results of local responsibility for the administration of education and states the case as follows:

For the European accustomed to centralized administration, control, and leadership in education it is difficult to realize that, in general, education is a local concern and that in localities, whether small rural districts or large and populous industrial cities, the control of education is often jealously guarded. Not only is there an almost complete absence, apart from slight exceptions, of federal direction and participation, but in most states the power of the central government also is very limited in the control of education. Even though education is legally a state function, its provision and administration are delegated to the localities, often with almost autonomous powers. Hence, education has become one of the most serious concerns as well as one of the largest undertakings of local governments. In the absence of strongly centralized and bureaucratic state administration of education the public locally has full freedom and opportunity to show its faith in education and to have the kind of education that is best suited to its needs.[30]

He finds it of great advantage that education should be based upon the interests and appreciations of the locality, and accordingly proposes:

First, that education should be largely a local affair, second, that it must have its roots in the local environment, third, that it cannot be cut to the same pattern over an extensive area. Education, except in so far as certain minimum standards are concerned in order to secure equality of opportunity, is not something that can be dictated from above. It must begin with the concerns of the

29 *Ibid.*, p. 413.   30 Kandel, I. L., *Essays in Comparative Education*, p. 56.

locality, with what the pupils bring to the school, and with what parents and public can appreciate. The teacher's task is to utilize this foundation for the full development of each pupil's personality, to make him into a fuller and richer member of society.[31]

In his discussion of the control of education in Germany, Kandel states clearly the area in which local initiative should be preserved:

Most German states have proceeded on the principle that culture is not one thing alone and that it is not subject to definition by authority. Accordingly, the function of the State is to provide those facilities that would lead to spontaneous development of national culture through the interplay of the individual and his environment. This explains the substitution of suggestions and outlines for prescribed courses of study. The tendency of the State is thus to allow some freedom and flexibility in the *interna* and to set up standards for the *externa*—buildings, size of classes, length of school term, and the qualifications and salaries of teachers.[32]

After quoting from John Stuart Mill on the fundamental theory underlying English education, he concludes:

It follows from this that State control is exercised through the annual grant which is distributed for educational purposes under conditions that set up general standards. But these conditions are concerned mainly with the *externa*—all those factors that make an efficient educative process possible. Through the grant the State is able to define standards for buildings and playgrounds, medical inspection, length of term, qualifications and remuneration of teachers, and the efficient organization of a coördinated system. The State refrains, however, from prescribing curricula and courses of study.[33]

Many laws have been passed in the United States dealing with the *interna*. The legislative enactments of individual states are, however, frequently permissive rather than mandatory, and often of an initiative rather than a regulatory character. Many of the school laws enacted during the past three decades have not gone beyond the stage of printers' ink, because of lack of power or effort to enforce their provisions.

It is evident from the foregoing discussion that the second criterion is linked up with the whole program and aim of education. Whether or not a tendency is concerned with *externa* or *interna* is of vital importance in a country which prides itself on the large degree of local responsibility which still exists in the administration of education. Thoughtful students of education

[31] Kandel, I. L., *Essays in Comparative Education*, pp. 73–74.   [32] *Ibid.*, p. 15.   [33] *Ibid.*, p. 19.

and legislators who would promote the welfare of the state
through education may not be unmindful of the issues raised by
this criterion.

III. *The educational program should be considered as a whole, and
special phases or types of education should not be supported at the
expense of the rest of the program.*

Special subsidies by either the federal or the state government
often single out some special aspect or feature of the educational
program. This favoritism does not always result in the handi-
capping of the remaining educational offerings, but it often estab-
lishes higher salaries, better school buildings and equipment, and
the like, for the particular undertaking. The most recent example is, of course, the work of the Federal Board for Vocational
Education.[34] Federal appropriations encourage this phase of the
public school curriculum, and the "matching" of federal contributions by the state deprives the state budget of funds that
might be utilized to support other kinds of training, and definitely
chains it to this special type of education. Emphasis upon this
training of those interested in agriculture, trade or industrial
occupations, and home economics is carried still further by the
provision of the Smith-Hughes Act permitting state boards for
vocational education to be created separate from all other established agencies of state educational administration.

Earlier examples of the aiding of special types of education
include the federal acts giving financial aid to colleges of agriculture and mechanic arts, agricultural experiment stations, and
navigation schools.[35]

The report of the National Advisory Committee on Education
finds that grants by the Federal Government tend to favor special
phases of education and thus throw the education program out of
balance:

> When special grants by the Federal Government are inaugurated as tempo-
> rary and transitional policies, in order to meet some apparent emergency of
> national importance, they tend to become permanent to a far greater degree
> than when made by state and local governments. . . .

[34] On October 10, 1933, the functions of the Federal Board for Vocational Education were
transferred to the Federal Office of Education in the Department of the Interior under the direction of Commissioner George F. Zook; this carries out the terms of the Executive order of June
10.

[35] For example, First Morrill Act, July 2, 1862; Hatch Act, March 2, 1887; State Marine
School Act, March 4, 1911.

Such federal favoring of special types of education obstructs the growing American tendency and aspiration to see and deal with the child's life and with society's needs as a balanced whole.[36]

In like manner, the several states have from time to time provided subsidies for special types of education. The intention in every case has been to promote some worthy phase of the educational program. The net result, however, has been to deprive the community of its responsibility to consider its needs as a whole. There is placed in the hands of the state authority control which may actually result in the denial of important educational opportunities. The third criterion must be acknowledged as significant if local initiative and local responsibility are considered desirable.

The character, the vitality, the ability to adapt itself to changing conditions, and at times the very existence of education in the several states have been an outgrowth of its decentralized administration and support. On the other hand, inequality of opportunity and, in recent years, even the absence of any opportunity have been associated with this same dependency upon the locality. It is important, therefore, to inquire concerning tendencies toward centralization and to discover, if possible, those which are essential to the realization of the broad social purpose of the state and those which interfere with the realization of the American ideal. In the succeeding chapters the centralizing tendencies in North Carolina, Maryland, and New York since 1900 will be discussed.

[36] National Advisory Committee on Education, *Federal Relations to Education*, Vol. I, p. 33.

CHAPTER II

CENTRALIZING TENDENCIES IN
THE ADMINISTRATION OF PUBLIC EDUCATION
IN NORTH CAROLINA

THE North Carolina Constitution of 1876 provided for an ex-officio State Board of Education, subordinate to the General Assembly, which was granted the power to amend or to replace the acts, rules, or regulations of the Board. The position of Superintendent of Public Instruction was also created, but the superintendent was not given the right to act as executive or administrative head of the State Board of Education. It was stipulated that the superintendent should be chosen by popular election, and no educational qualifications were specified for the position. These and other detailed provisions regarding a system of public education did much to retard the tendencies toward centralization in the administration of the educational facilities of the state.

STATE SUPPORT

One of the outstanding centralizing tendencies which has manifested itself in North Carolina during the thirty-three-year period under consideration is that of financial support. As the following quotation indicates, state support in 1901 was based partially on the size of the school population, for the purpose of aiding each school district in the state to maintain schools for the four months' term prescribed by the state constitution:

That the sum of one hundred thousand dollars ($100,000) be and the same is hereby appropriated, annually, out of the State treasury for the benefit of the public schools, to be distributed to the respective counties of the State (per capita) as to school population on the first Monday in January of each year, using the school census of the previous scholastic year as a basis of apportionment.[1]

That the sum of one hundred thousand dollars ($100,000), or so much thereof as may be necessary, be and the same is hereby appropriated annually

---

[1] *Public Laws of North Carolina*, 1901, Chap. 543, Sec. 1. Hereafter referred to in the footnotes of this chapter as *P. L. of N. C.*

out of the State treasury for the purpose of bringing up to the constitutional requirement for a four months' public school term in each school district in the State, those public schools whose terms, after the distribution and application of all other school funds, do not comply with said requirement, to be distributed and applied in the manner hereinafter set forth.[2]

The State Board of Education shall, on the first Monday in August of each and every year, apportion among the several counties of the State all the school funds which may be then in the treasury of the said board, and order a warrant for the full apportionment to each county, which said apportionment shall be made on the basis of the school population; but no part of the permanent school fund shall be apportioned or distributed, but only the income therefrom.[3]

The requirement that a special tax should be levied in counties where the regular tax plus the state aid was insufficient to maintain one or more schools for a four months' term in each district was passed by the General Assembly in 1901:

If the tax levied for the State for the support of the public schools shall be insufficient to maintain one or more schools in each school district for the period of four months, then the Board of Commissioners of each county shall levy annually a special tax to supply the deficiency for the support and maintenance of said schools for the said period of four months or more. . . . But the County Board of Education shall not be required to expend upon a district containing less than sixty-five pupils the same sum it may give to larger districts, notwithstanding an inequality of length of school terms may be the result. . . .[4]

This law was badly needed and it took several years to carry out its provisions. Three years later, according to a study by the General Education Board, we find that

Of the 97 counties at that time, 30 had a school term of less than four months, 51 between four and five months, 13 between five and six months, 1 between six and seven months, and 2 a school term of more than seven months.[5]

Many of the county boards apparently considered the constitutional provision and the law passed at the 1901 session of the General Assembly to be permissive rather than mandatory. The matter finally reached the Supreme Court of the state and in the decision, Collie vs. Commissioners of Franklin County, in 1907,[6] it was decided that the four months' term was mandatory and that each county must levy whatever tax was necessary on all property and polls to keep the schools open for the minimum term established by the state constitution. This was a very important

[2] P. L. of N. C., 1901, Chap. 543, Sec. 3.   [3] Ibid., Chap. 4, Sec. 1.   [4] Ibid., Sec. 6.
[5] General Education Board, Public Education in North Carolina, p. 25.
[6] North Carolina Reports, 1907, Vol. 145, p. 170.

ruling both because of the responsibility that it placed on the county officials and because of the added authority that it gave to the other stipulations of the constitution dealing with public education.

The effort to discourage small school districts by penalizing them in the distribution of funds was continued in 1903 by incorporating in the law governing the distribution of state monies the following section:

> That no school with a school census of less than sixty-five shall receive any benefit under this act unless the formation and continuance of such district shall have been for good and sufficient reasons, to-wit, sparsity of population or peculiar geographical conditions, such as intervening streams, swamps or mountains, said reasons to be set forth in an affidavit by the chairman of the County Board of Education and the County Superintendent of Schools, and to be approved by the State Superintendent of Public Instruction.[7]

North Carolina is largely a rural state and as late as 1903 modern methods of transportation were not available.   State Superintendent Joyner in his biennial report for 1901 and 1902 states that "since June 30, 1901, 318 districts have been consolidated and there has been a total decrease of 179 districts."[8]   He also points out that despite this progress toward the elimination of the less populated districts through consolidation,

> the reports of County Superintendents show that 47 per cent, nearly one-half, of the white school districts of the State, and 44 per cent of the colored districts contain less than sixty-five children of school age, the minimum fixed by law.[9]

Not all the trends at the beginning of the century were of a centralizing nature.   Permissive legislation passed by the 1901 session of the General Assembly allowed the formation of special tax districts.   There was some question concerning the legality of such districts, but the 1903 session held that the act of the 1901 session was legal,[10] and a decision of the Supreme Court in 1906 upheld it. This was a very unfortunate occurrence from the standpoint of maintaining or increasing the importance of the county unit which had been made a part of the detailed provisions for public education in the constitution of 1876.   Wealthy sections all over the state organized themselves as special tax districts for school purposes.   The opinion expressed in the report made by the General Education Board is as follows:

[7] P. L. of N. C., 1903, Chap. 751, Sec. 7.
[8] Biennial Report of the Superintendent of Public Instruction of North Carolina, 1902, p. xxii.
[9] Ibid., p. xxi.   [10] P. L. of N. C., 1903, Chap. 614, Sec. 1.

The law of 1901 removed all limits on the bounds that the county board of education might set for a special tax district. With this freedom and under the impelling desire to secure better schools, the school districts in most counties have been gerrymandered beyond relief. Special tax district lines include or exclude farms, according as the owner is favorable or unfavorable; they extend far up and down railroads, and far up and down rich river valleys—anywhere to enclose taxable property, particularly of corporations, that may accrue to the benefit of the particular district.[11]

This formation of new districts on the basis of property values caused the county system, for the time being, to be of little value in bringing about equal educational opportunities for all the children of the state. The limitations placed on teachers' salaries paid by districts applying for financial aid enabled the small amount of money available to be spent to the best advantage — to help those districts that needed it the most.[12]

State Superintendent Joyner, with the aid of funds from the General Education Board, the Peabody Fund, the Slater Fund, and the campaign for local taxation to support part of the school costs, brought about increased interest in public education among the citizens of North Carolina and their representatives in the General Assembly. The 1909 session of the Assembly enacted a law appropriating $125,000 annually to the counties to be distributed per capita as to school population, "using the school census of the previous scholastic year as a basis of apportionment."[13] The same session also set aside $100,000 with the following proviso:

. . . the money shall be placed by said treasurer to the credit of the general public school fund of the county, to be used, first, for providing a four months' school term in every school district, and any balance to be used for equalizing as nearly as may be, the terms of all the public schools of said county.[14]

The amount of money was too small to begin to equalize the terms of the schools within the average county, but its provision was the continuation of the plan begun in 1901 to equalize the burden of taxes among the counties.

Encouraged by the increasing public participation and support, the Assembly voted at an extra session in 1913 to amend the four months' term as required by the constitution of 1876 and to require instead a term of six months. Although the necessary three-fifths vote of each house of the General Assembly was secured, the

---

amendment failed to poll the necessary majority when it was submitted to the people of the state.[15]   The "State Equalizing School Fund" was created by the regular session of the 1913 state legislature to be raised by means of an annual ad valorem tax to be levied on real and personal property.   Among the provisions of the fund were the following:

> There shall be set aside annually five cents of the annual (ad valorem) tax levied and collected for State purposes on every one hundred dollars value of real and personal property in this State, and the funds annually arising from said tax shall be held by the State Treasurer as a fund separate and apart from all other funds for State purposes, and shall be known as "The State Equalizing School Fund," and shall be used as hereinafter directed to provide a six months' school term in every school district in the State, or as nearly a six months' term as said funds will provide.[16]

> . . . The State Board of Education, however, shall apportion this fund only for the salaries of the teachers employed. . . .[17]

> . . . No county shall receive any part of the State equalizing school fund provided by this act until it shall have levied the special tax herein required of it for a four months' school term in every school district.[18]

It was not until after the session of 1917 had repeated the action of amending the constitutional school term[19] that the voters of the state finally brought about the change in the length of term at the general election in 1918.   At the next session of the General Assembly, in 1919, a tax of 32 cents on every $100 of valuation of taxable property was levied for the maintenance of the public schools.   County boards were required to submit their budgets to the State Board of Education and to levy a special county school tax to make possible a six months' school term in every school district.[20]   A State Tax Commission was formed and the new school law included the proviso that

> . . . after the school year 1919–1920 the county board of education shall submit to the State Board of Education together with the county budget, a certificate from the State Tax Commission to the effect that the property of said county has been assessed in accordance with the provisions of law.[21]

Inequality in the determination of assessed valuations results in unequal tax burdens, and this proviso was an attempt to eliminate this factor of unfairness.

---

[15] P. L. of N. C., Extra Session, 1913, Chap. 81, Sec. 1.   [16] P. L. of N. C., 1913, Chap. 33, Sec. 3.
[17] Ibid., Sec. 4.   [18] Ibid., Sec. 8.
[19] P. L. of N. C., 1917, Chap. 192, Sec. 1.   [20] P. L. of N. C., 1919, Chap. 102, Sec. 1 and 5.
[21] Ibid., Chap. 102, Sec. 4.

Despite the progress already made in the consolidation of districts there was scope for continued action along this line. The 1919 legislature sought to bring about larger districts by providing that

The apportionment of the State Public School Fund shall be administered so as to encourage consolidation of districts and the elimination of small schools or small districts. . . .[22]

Since salaries are usually the largest single item in the budget of a school district, the following provision of the Public Laws of 1919 was received with enthusiasm by the county boards of education:

Out of said funds the State Board of Education shall apportion annually to each county of the State, on or before the first day of January of each and every year, a sum sufficient to pay one-half the annual salary of the county superintendent and three months' salary of all teachers of all sorts employed in the public schools of the county, including the teachers of city, town, township, and all special chartered schools, and one-third the annual salary of all city superintendents: (Provided), that no part of this fund shall be used to pay the salaries of teachers that receive appropriations from other State funds.[23]

The salaries of teachers holding second-grade certificates issued by counties and cities were increased from $35 to $45, while teachers having state certificates received from 10 to 25 per cent salary increments.[24] Some idea of the need for additional funds for public education may be had from the fact that the average annual salaries of rural elementary teachers for the school year 1919–1920 were $430 for white teachers and $295 for colored teachers.[25] The extra session of 1920 used the equalizing fund as a lever to force the counties to raise additional funds:

. . . no county shall participate in the equalizing fund until it shall have provided by tax levy ten (10%) per cent more for the school year one thousand nine hundred and twenty and one thousand nine hundred and twenty-one than it provided in the school year one thousand nine hundred and nineteen and one thousand nine hundred and twenty.[26]

The "State Public School Fund" was made up of an annual appropriation of $1,400,000 by act of the 1921 legislature.[27] This fund was used to supplement the county funds in providing six

[22] P. L. of N. C., 1919, Chap. 102, Sec. 9.   [23] Ibid., Chap. 102, Sec. 2.
[24] Ibid., Chap. 114, Sec. 2.   [25] Public Education in North Carolina, op. cit., p. 48.
[26] P. L. of N. C., Extra Session, 1920, Chap. 91, Sec. 2.   [27] P. L. of N. C., 1921, Chap. 146, Sec. 1.

months' terms for all schools. The final authority in the matter of the amount needed to maintain schools for six months was the jury of the superior court of each county. The county commissioners were ordered by the extra session of 1921 to levy taxes in accordance with the judgment of the superior court jury.[28]

Not all of the money spent for school purposes had come from current taxes. Bonds and notes had been issued by many of the districts, cities, and counties. Some of these financial obligations had not been carried out — defaults of both interest and principal had occurred.[29] The extra session in 1921 set out to remedy the situation through the enactment of a law compelling the county, township, school district, or municipality issuing bonds or notes to file complete information in regard to them with the State Auditor.[30]

The State Educational Commission created by the General Assembly of 1917 made a survey of the educational system with the help of the state officials and the General Education Board. The report of the Commission was submitted to the General Assembly of 1921. One of the greatest changes made by the 1921 legislature was the provision for an annual audit of the books of the treasurers of the county school funds and the accounts of the county boards of education.[31] It was provided that the auditor's report should include facts on taxes, the state and county six months' school fund, salaries paid, and the building fund, and a comparison of the expenditures with the approved budget. This was indeed a transfer of authority from a smaller to a larger unit of administration. Arrangement was also made whereby audits were required of city school districts unless they were exempted by a special act of the Assembly. Failure of the county superintendent to keep his records so that they could be audited might bring about the revocation of his certificate by the State Board of Education.

The equalizing fund was apportioned to each county in 1923 on the basis of the average amount needed to pay the salaries of all teachers and principals for the six months' term for the school years 1921–1922 and 1922–1923, minus the gross yield of the legal tax rate of the county for the six months' term. Each county entitled to share in the equalizing fund was also to receive one-half

[28] P. L. of N. C., Extra Session, 1921, Chap. 93, Sec. 1.   [29] Ibid., Foreword to Chap. 1.
[30] Ibid ., Chap. 1, Sec. 1.   [31] P. L. of N. C., 1921, Chap. 236.

the salary of the county superintendent up to one-half the salary listed on the state salary schedule.[32]   This method of distribution of funds was a forerunner of the State Salary Schedule.

The General Assembly of 1927 enacted a law concerning the detail of the county budgets, stating that they should set up three separate school funds — current expense, capital outlay, and debt service.   The Assembly also listed the items to be included in each fund.[33]   This act made it possible to compare the budget of one county with the budget of another and it enabled the state authorities to check more closely on expenditures for education within the state.   The attempt to secure some degree of stand-ardization in accounting for funds spent for public education went still further in 1929 with the following power delegated to the "County Government Advisory Commission":

> That with a view of standardization and simplification of the methods of accounting in the various counties of the State, the County Government Advisory Commission is hereby authorized and empowered to advise with said boards as to the proper methods of accounting for such counties and no system or books shall be installed until same shall have been submitted to the County Government Advisory Commission.[34]

Before any county participated in the equalizing fund for the school years 1929–1930 and 1930–1931, a tax of 30 cents on each $100 of valuation was to be levied by the Board of County Com-missioners.   The State Board of Equalization was empowered to determine the valuation of each county.[35]   The sum of $1,250,000 was voted for state aid, with the following method of distribution:

> . . . the additional sum of one million two hundred fifty thousand dollars ($1,250,000), to be known as the tax reduction fund, shall be apportioned by the State Board of Equalization to the participating counties on the following ratio or basis: There shall be apportioned to each participating county, as near as may be, the same percentage of current expense funds, calculated according to State standards, of the combined school districts having extended term as said county receives of its approved budget from the Equalizing Fund for the six months' term.[36]

This tax reduction fund was intended to aid in extending the length of term throughout the state two months beyond the constitutional six months' term.   It followed the general trend of increasing the amount of financial support for schools raised

---

[32] *P. L. of N. C.*, 1923, Chap. 141, Sec. 3 and 4.   [33] *P. L. of N. C.*, 1927, Chap. 239, Sec. 2.
[34] *P. L. of N. C.*, 1929, Chap. 201, Sec. 3.   [35] *Ibid.*, Chap. 245, Sec. 5.
[36] *Ibid.*, Chap. 245, Sec. 30.

on a state-wide basis and of decreasing the proportion of the total school funds raised by local taxation. This extended term was financed on the district basis and state aid went only to districts voting for the extended term a special tax of 15 cents on each $100 of valuation. The 1931 General Assembly passed an act making the six months' term mandatory and providing that it should "be maintained by the state from sources other than ad valorem taxation on property" [37]; the purpose was stated thus:

> That this provision of the Constitution is mandatory and that legislation will be enacted by this General Assembly to make it effective, so that the public school system for the constitutional term of at least six months shall be general and uniform in all the counties and shall be maintained by the State from sources other than ad valorem taxation on property.[38]

The principle of equalization of assessed valuations was carried into the individual counties and the Board of County Commissioners of each county was constituted the Board of Equalization and Review for its own county. The tentative list was made up by the County Supervisor of Taxation and submitted to the State Board of Equalization and Review.[39] This effort to secure more equitable assessments strengthened the county government and decreased the influence of the local units within the county borders. The school law was modified to permit the levying of a 15-cent ad valorem tax when the 1931 General Assembly could not agree on indirect taxes yielding sufficient revenue.

The extended term was financed in the same way that it had been in the past with the State Board of Equalization determining the property values in the districts and fixing a uniform tax rate which each district wishing to have an extended term had to levy. State aid for the districts voting a local tax for the extended term was provided, as it had been before, from the Tax Reduction Fund.[40] This fund was $1,500,000 for each year of the biennium 1931–1933. Counties could vote and levy supplementary taxes for the six months' school term.[41] Cities could raise additional funds with the consent of the voters to support the six months' term more adequately or to raise monies for the extended term.

The School Machinery Act of 1933 extended the state support of public schools to include an eight months' term instead of a six

[37] P. L. of N. C., 1931, Chap. 10, Sec. 1.   [38] Ibid., Chap. 10, Sec. 1.
[39] Ibid., Chap. 428, Sec. 523 (1).   [40] Ibid., Chap. 440, Sec. 1.
[41] Ibid., Chap. 430, Sec. 15.

months' term. A 3 per cent general sales tax was levied to provide the necessary monies. The state was given complete control of the county and city school budgets with power to prepare statements of cost and have general supervision of the operation of the schools. A State School Commission was established in place of the State Board of Equalization and was authorized to re-district the state in the interests of economy, altering truck routes whenever necessary. Administrative units were ruled to be of two types—the county unit and the city unit. Supplementary taxes could be levied in administrative units only, for the regular eight months' school term, upon a favorable vote by the people of the administrative unit concerned, but no term might be longer than 180 days. Counties were allowed to levy taxes for teaching vocational agriculture and home economics— matching appropriations of the Federal Government for these purposes.

Section 8 of the 1933 Act provides that no funds shall be allotted for rural supervisors, that the amount of money paid to school attendance officers shall be decided by the State School Commission, and that privately donated funds may be used for whatever purpose the State School Commission designates.

Section 11 carries the proviso that the employment of teachers shall not depend upon their marital status. Section 12 places upon the State Board of Education and the State School Commission the duty of drawing up a State Standard Salary Schedule for teachers and principals—said schedule to be in terms of the maximum salaries to be paid from the State Education Fund by the administrative unit. The checking of the operating budgets of the administrative units by the State School Commission in accordance with Section 19 and the auditing of all school funds required by Section 21 insure control by the state authorities over the expenditures for public education.

A method of conducting an eight months' school term in six months was suggested by Section 15, by permitting the school week to be lengthened from five days to six or the school day to be extended by an hour of instructional service subject to the approval of the State School Commission. In the event of such action by the local school authorities, the State School Commission was given the power to adjust teachers' salaries to cover this additional instructional service.

Evaluation in Terms of the Criteria

North Carolina has gone a long way in the financing of public education during the past three decades. Beginning with the equalization fund of 1900 and ending with the state support of the eight months' term in 1933, there has been a long difficult fight against poverty, a scattered school population, public indifference, and a division of authority and responsibility for the operation of the public school system throughout the state. The recent changes in the methods of financing the schools of the state have shorn the localities of their powers. An election must be held in order to levy any local tax for school purposes, schools may not be kept open for more than 180 days, teachers may not be paid from the State Education Fund more than the state salary schedule, and detailed operating budgets must be approved by state authorities. Centralization of the financing of education in North Carolina has been carried to the extreme of setting up maxima rather than minima; of deciding by state officials how every dollar shall be spent; and the plan of complete state support rather than state aid has rendered it extremely difficult for any administrative unit to spend more than the state support provides. One of the problems at the beginning of the century was to persuade local tax districts to levy a tax raising sufficient funds to conduct a public school for four months. At present schools are supported by the state for eight months and local taxation for school purposes is decidedly discouraged. This change from state aid to complete state support has been brought about largely because of difficulties which have been encountered in recent years in financing the schools in a time of economic distress. Whether or not this step will remain a permanent measure after economic recovery comes about will depend upon the way in which the present arrangement works out and what plans are made for the raising of other necessary revenues for government services.

This tendency toward centralization in the financing of public education has, year by year, seen the transfer of responsibility and authority from the many types of districts which have been established in the state during the present century to the various state agencies which have been created from time to time. None of the state boards or commissions which have been established have been under the direct control of the State Board of Education. Thus, while certain powers have been transferred to state authorities, this action has not resulted in the heading up of all the educational functions by a single executive or by one board or commission. At the same time, the financial independence of the units of administration within the state has largely been surrendered to the state authorities. The special tax districts which flourished during the first decade of the century, with the exception of the city districts, have been eliminated. Section 4 of the School Machinery Act of 1933 provides, however, that special districts having financial obligations shall be maintained until taxes have been levied and collected for payment of the indebtedness, unless said indebtedness has been taken over by the county. Those special districts maintained to pay off existing obligations are then abolished as school districts.

What has been the probable effect of these changes in the financing of education upon the school children of North Carolina? To answer this question we turn to the evaluation of the centralizing tendency found in school financing in the light of our criteria.

The complete state support of the eight months' school term, by means of the general sales tax and other state taxes and revenues if necessary, furnishes every child in the state with equal educational opportunities up to the minimum established by the state. The direct administration of the schools is placed in the hands of the State School Commission rather than in the State Department of Education, so the principle of having one controlling body is not fulfilled.

How does the centralization that has taken place in financing public schools affect the opportunity for local initiative and experimentation? Certain of the state requirements which have been legislated are expressed in terms of maxima rather than minima. The state salary schedule has been determined on the basis of maximum salaries that can be paid from the State Education Fund. Budgets must be constructed with not more than a certain number of principals for a given number of teachers, and the State School Commission has the power to limit the number of elementary and high school teachers to be included in the state budget. The supplementing of state budget allotments entails the holding of an election in the administrative unit concerned, but even after voting additional funds no unit is allowed to provide a term of more than 180 days.[42] Because several

42 *P. L. of N. C.*, 1933, Sec. 17.

of the state controls are maximum rather than minimum limitations, the tendency is regarded unfavorably in the light of the second criterion.

Financial support, in and of itself, is one of the *externa* of education. Sometimes it is used as a means of controlling certain *interna* of education. In North Carolina it has been the means of standardizing certain *externa*, for example, the length of term, minimum requirements for school employees, and salary schedules. Centralization of the financing of the public school system of North Carolina has also given the state control over many of the *interna*. The control exercised by the State School Commission in eliminating or curtailing items of expenditure of local budgets operates to affect matters of *interna*.

The change in policy in 1931 and 1933, providing for state support rather than state aid, eliminated the state grants for specific parts of the educational program. The "matching" of the federal appropriations is provided for by permitting counties to levy taxes for this purpose. It is estimated by Superintendent A. T. Allen that this tax will amount to about $350,000, not a large sum when compared with the state appropriation of $16,000,000.

Special subsidies are not justified according to the third criterion. The changes which have taken place in North Carolina have eliminated all the special subsidies granted by the state, substituting budgetary control to insure expenditures of administrative units in accord with the policies of the State School Commission.

BUILDINGS

The school buildings of North Carolina have changed greatly during the past three decades. The materials of construction, the method of lighting, the shape and size, and the suitability of the various spaces provided in the building for school purposes have all improved under the leadership of the state authorities. This action has come about not swiftly nor easily but only after the provision of inspection of plans by the state and the continued supplying of loan funds to the local units for building and repairing. The 1903 General Assembly provided:

. . . The building of all new school houses shall be under the control and direction of and by contract with the County Board of Education: . . . (Provided further), that they shall not be authorized to invest any money in any new

house that is not built in accordance with plans approved by the State Superintendent of Public Instruction and the County Board of Education, and that
all contracts for buildings shall be in writing and all buildings shall be inspected,
reviewed, and approved by the County Superintendent of Public Instruction
before full payment is made therefor.[43]

This action placed responsibility for the building of new schools
in the county boards. The final responsibility for approval was
also vested in the county boards. And yet the approval of the
plans by both the state superintendent and the county board was
not as valuable a requirement as might be supposed. The staff
of the state superintendent was so inadequate at this time that
it was impossible for his office to attend to all the details connected
with the enforcement of the laws entrusted to it.

The same session of the legislature also set up a plan for the
lending of funds by the state to the county boards of education
for the building and improving of public school plants. Arrangement was also made whereby the county boards could lend
the funds supplied them by the state to the districts within each
county. The plan provided:

That all funds of the State heretofore derived from the sources enumerated in
Section four, Article nine of the State Constitution, and all funds that may be
hereafter so derived, together with any interest that may accrue thereon, shall
be a fund separate and distinct from the other funds of the State, to be known
as the State Literary Fund.[44]

That the State Board of Education under such rules and regulations as it
may deem advisable, not inconsistent with the provisions of this act, may make
loans from such fund to the County Board of Education of any county for the
building and improving of public school-houses in such county.[45]

That the County Board of Education, from any sum borrowed under the
provisions of this act, may make loans to any district in such county for the
purpose of building school-houses in such districts and the amount so loaned to
any district shall be payable in ten annual installments, with interest thereon
at four per cent., payable annually.[46]

An additional check on the plans for new school buildings was
created in 1909, when it was decided that all plans for public
buildings should be submitted to the State Insurance Commissioner for examination as to the safety of proposed buildings.
This measure was of special importance at that time because
of the large number of wooden schoolhouses and the inadequate

[43] *P. L. of N. C.*, 1903, Chap. 435, Sec. 4.   [44] *Ibid.*, Chap. 567, Sec. 1.
[45] *Ibid.*, Sec. 2.   [46] *Ibid.*, Sec. 5.

means of fire-fighting available in the buildings and in the communities which they served.   The plan authorized that

. . . No board, commission, superintendent, or other person or persons authorized and directed by law to select plans and erect buildings for the use of the State of North Carolina or any institution thereof shall receive and approve of any plans until they are submitted to and approved by the Insurance Commissioner of the State as to the safety of the proposed buildings from fire, as well as the protection of the inmates in case of fire.[47]

The increasing number of children attending school, the movement toward consolidation by building schools to serve larger areas, and the cheap construction of many of the structures already erected made it necessary to provide means for greater expenditure for construction purposes.   The 1919 General Assembly made it possible for the county boards of education, with the approval of the county commissioners, to increase the budget by an amount not to exceed one-fourth of the teachers' salary fund.   It was also made permissible to increase the county tax rate beyond the 35 cents maximum levy established by law:

All poll tax, fines, forfeitures, penalties, and all public school revenues, other than that derived from the State Public School Fund and the special county tax, shall be placed to the credit of the incidental expense fund and the building fund, as provided in the budget, and if this amount is insufficient for these funds, the county board of education may provide in the county school budget for an additional amount not to exceed twenty-five per cent of the teachers' salary fund, and the county tax may be increased sufficiently beyond the maximum levy of thirty-five cents to provide this amount if it shall appear necessary to the county board of education and the county commissioners.[48]

The same session set aside the sum of $2,000 annually for drawing up school building plans to be given to the districts, for inspecting school buildings, for inspecting the use of state funds, and for any other uses that the State Board of Education might consider would make for better buildings or more intelligent use of the monies lent by the state: [49]

. . . The State Board of Education may annually set aside and use out of the funds accruing to the interest of said State Loan Fund a sum not exceeding two thousand dollars, to be used for providing plans for modern school buildings to be furnished free of charge to districts, for providing proper inspection of school buildings and the use of State funds, and for such other purposes as said board may determine, to secure the erection of a better type of school buildings and the better administration of said State Loan Fund.[50]

[47] *P. L. of N. C.*, 1909, Chap. 880, Sec. 1.   [48] *P. L. of N. C.* 1919, Chap. 102, Sec. 7.
[49] *P. L. of N. C.* Special Session, 1920, Chap. 91, Sec. 6.   [50] *P. L. of N. C.*, 1919, Chap. 254, Sec. 21.

The General Assembly of 1921, following the recommendation of the State Educational Commission, created by the General Assembly of 1917, appropriated $10,000 a year to finance a "Division of Schoolhouse Planning." This step recognized the need of greater facilities to enable the state authorities to exercise the powers granted them, and it helped the state to extend its inspection of plans and buildings throughout the state.

The funds which had been provided as loans to the counties to aid in erecting buildings were insufficient, and in 1921 a law was passed authorizing a five-million-dollar state bond issue to raise a Special Building Fund. This building fund was to be lent by the State Board of Education to the county boards for "building, equipping, and repairing public school buildings, dormitories, teacherages, and for the purchase of suitable sites." [51] It was further provided that

. . . no loan shall be made from this fund for erecting or repairing any school building containing less than five rooms, nor shall any building be erected in whole or in part from funds borrowed from the State unless the plans for said building shall have been approved by the State Superintendent of Public Instruction. [52]

This building fund was provided with another five million dollars in 1923 [53] and still a third five million dollars in 1925. [54]

The General Assembly of 1925, in order to insure that buildings should be erected or repaired according to the plans approved by the State Board of Education, enacted a permissive plan whereby the board could withhold 15 per cent of the loan until the completed building was finally found satisfactory by the board or its agent:

. . . From any moneys loaned by the State to any one of the several counties for the erection, repair, or equipment of school buildings, teacherages and dormitories, the State Board of Education, under such rules as it may deem advisable, not inconsistent with the provisions of this article, may retain an amount not to exceed 15 per cent of the said loan until such completed buildings, erected or repaired, in whole or in part, from such loan funds, shall have been approved by such agent as the State Board of Education may designate: (Provided), that upon the proper approval of the completed building, the State Treasurer, upon requisition of the State Superintendent of Public Instruction, authorized and directed by the State Board of Education, shall pay to the treasurer of the county the remaining part of said loan, together with interest

[51] *P. L. of N. C.*, 1921, Chap. 147, Sc. 3.   [52] *Ibid.*
[53] *P. L. of N. C.*, 1923, Chap. 136, Art. 25.   [54] *P. L. of N. C.*, 1925, Chap. 201, Sec. 1.

from the date of the loan at a rate not less than 3 per cent on monthly balances.[55]

The 1927 legislature directed the raising of $2,500,000 by a state bond issue to supply monies for a special building fund. The stipulation was made that no loans should be made until the plans had been approved by the State Superintendent of Public Instruction. Loans were limited to the erection or the repair of buildings of seven rooms or more—thus discouraging, as did the original special building fund act in 1921, the construction or maintenance of small neighborhood schools.[56]

It is impossible to calculate the effect that this centralization of planning and support of schoolhouse construction has had upon the public schools of the state. There is no way of comparing what the situation would be today if local option, or even county control, had held sway, with the results which have been achieved under the direction of the state. Uniformity in the planning and construction of buildings is considered desirable by most educational leaders, and the method of financing building construction and repairs in North Carolina enabled the communities needing funds to secure them at a lower rate of interest than would otherwise have been the case.

Evaluation in Terms of the Criteria

This centralization of authority in regard to the planning and construction of public school buildings carries out the principles of equalization of educational opportunity and equalization of school support, as defined in the chapter on criteria. Minimum qualifications have been drawn up to control the buildings erected, thus helping to bring about equal educational opportunities, so far as buildings are concerned, for all children in all parts of the state. The funds for operating the Division of Schoolhouse Planning come from state taxes, and the monies in the special loan funds lent to the counties for building and repairing purposes are raised by means of state bond issues.

The standards established for building repair and construction are minimum in nature, and local initiative and experimentation are given some opportunity to function. A limit is placed on the taxes which a locality may levy, so full freedom for local initiative is not provided. Maintenance of local initiative is not so im-

[55] *P. L. of N. C.*, 1925, Chap. 221, Sec. 1.   [56] *P. L. of N. C.*, 1927, Chap. 199, Sec. 1.

portant in the matter of buildings as it is in such aspects of the school as the curriculum, methods of teaching, or other *interna*. The control of the planning of buildings helps to prevent the construction of wasteful, dangerous, or poorly conceived structures. Inasmuch as this tendency does not prevent local communities from carrying out plans for buildings better than those suggested by the state plans, opportunity for local initiative is maintained up to the point where the locality encounters the restriction on the amount of money that may be spent for this purpose.

The definitions given in the chapter on criteria include hygienic buildings among the *externa* of education. Good buildings are considered one of the conditions essential to good education, one of the factors that make possible an efficient educative process. Since the tendency relates to one of the *externa* of education it is acceptable under the second criterion.

No differentiation has been made, in lending funds or in passing on plans, between types of buildings within the public school system. All types of buildings, including teacherages, are equally eligible to receive loans from the state fund and the plans of all buildings must be submitted to the State Department of Education. The state fund is not a special subsidy to encourage a special part of the educational program, and since the money is lent and not granted, and the expenditure is for capital outlay purposes, it is expected that the major portion of it will find its way back to the state treasury.

THE CURRICULUM

The state course of study in 1901 included, according to the state law,

. . . orthography, defining, writing, drawing, arithmetic, geography, grammar, language lessons, history of North Carolina, including the Constitution of the state, history of the United States, including Constitution of the United States, physiology, hygiene, nature and effect of alcoholic drinks and narcotics, elements of civil government, elements of agriculture, theory and practice of teaching, and such other branches as the State Board of Education may direct.[57]

These subjects were required to be taught in every public school in the state; the large number of one- and two-teacher schools,

---

[57] *P. L. of N. C.*, 1901, Chap. 4, Sec. 37.

however, made compliance with the law a physical impossibility. In the same year, October 12 was designated as North Carolina Day, with the requirement that schools should consider on that occasion "some topic or topics of North Carolina History selected by the Superintendent of Public Instruction."[58] In addition to the law listing the specific fields of knowledge to be included in the curriculum, there was another dealing with the avoidance of sectarian doctrine,[59] and a third having to do with the desired social and ethical outcomes of public schooling.[60] Since there were no state inspectors or supervisors to follow the fate or check on the enforcement of these laws, no data are available on which to form an opinion concerning the number of school districts, large and small, in various parts of the state which departed from these legislative enactments in the composition and teaching of their respective courses of study.   Even if there had been a means of checking on the observance of the state course of study, there was little that could have been done to enforce the will of the state. The fund available for state aid to education at that time was very small and so widely distributed that withholding the appropriation in any given locality would, in most cases, have been insufficient to bring about the installation of the state-legislated curriculum.

As the state contributions to education increased, there soon arose the question of payment for instruction in subject matter not mentioned specifically in the school law.   This was decided in 1905 by the regular session of the General Assembly, which decreed that other subjects than those included in the state curriculum might receive the support of the state aid distributed.[61]

The teaching of physiology and hygiene was required by law in 1901, but in 1907 the group or groups interested succeeded in passing an act calling for the use of a textbook for teaching these subjects.[62]

The most radical change in the matter of subjects to be taught came in 1921 with the passage of a measure designed to meet the conditions set up under the Smith-Hughes Act for Vocational Education.[63]   This measure established the teaching and financial support of this special type of education on a new basis.

[58] P. L. of N. C., 1901, Chap. 164.   [59] Ibid., Chap. 1, Sec. 2.
[60] Ibid., Chap. 4, Sec. 63.   [61] P. L. of N. C., 1905, Chap. 533, Sec. 12.
[62] P. L. of N. C., 1907, Chap. 835, Sec. 1-C.   [63] P. L. of N. C., 1921, Chap. 146, Sec. 1-3.

North Carolina, in reaching eagerly for the federal subsidy, had to agree under the law to devote a like amount of state funds to the same purpose, a proviso which operated to decrease the state funds available for general educational purposes. There was set up a new State Vocational Education Board concerned solely with the oversight of this limited part of the educational field.

It was assumed that the teaching of patriotism and loyalty should be intermingled with the teaching of the required school subjects, especially history, geography, and kindred subjects. Enough interest was stirred up in 1923, however, to cause the passage of a law requiring a course in "Americanism" to be taught not less than thirty hours a year.[64] The duty of selecting the proper textbook was delegated to the State Board of Education and the state superintendent was asked to prepare the outlines for the courses of study.

The list of subjects required by the 1901 ordinance concluded with the following phrase, "and such other branches as the State Board of Education may direct." [65] Twenty-two years later a somewhat similar list of subjects was written into the education law. This new list began, "County board shall provide for teaching of following in all seven-year elementary schools," and ended, "These subjects to be taught in English."[66] The responsibility for carrying out this course of study still remained with the State Board of Education.

Other laws passed in 1923 affecting the course of study had to do with music,[67] social and ethical outcomes,[67] physical examinations,[68] temperance day,[69] constitutions of North Carolina and the United States, and patriotism,[70] and Arbor Day[71] which had already been provided for in 1919.

The teaching of the nature and effect of alcoholic drinks and narcotics was first required by statute in 1901. It was included again in the list of subjects required by law in 1923. The requirement was made more specific in 1929 by the legal regulation that in any one grade in any one year there should be a minimum of ten lessons on the effects of alcoholism and narcotism on the human system.[72]

[64] P. L. of N. C., 1923, Chap. 49, Sec. 1–5.   [65] P. L. of N. C., 1901, Chap. 4, Sec. 37.
[66] P. L. of N. C., 1923, Chap. 136, Sec. 39.   [67] Ibid., Sec. 165.
[68] Ibid., Sec. 170.   [69] Ibid., Sec. 368.
[70] Ibid., Chap. 49.   [71] Ibid., Chap. 136, Sec. 369.
[72] Supplement to North Carolina Code, 1929, Sec. 5540a.

Physiology and hygiene were included in the list of subjects that comprised the state course of study in 1901.   The General Assembly of 1907 made mandatory the use of a textbook for teaching physiology and hygiene.   The Laws of 1923 listed health as one of the subjects to be taught state-wide.   The Supplement to the North Carolina Code for 1929 raises health to a still more important level by requiring that in all normal schools, teacher training classes, and summer schools "time and attention be given to methods of teaching health education . . . those failing to comply are subject to dismissal."[73]

The determination of the textbooks which are to be used is one of the most certain ways of influencing the curriculum.   In 1919 the General Assembly of North Carolina passed an act to secure uniformity of high school textbooks within each county.   It provided that the State Superintendent of Public Instruction should prepare a list of approved textbooks and that a committee in each county should select a county list from the list issued by the state superintendent.[74]

The State Board of Education was authorized in 1921 to adopt textbooks for use in all the public elementary schools in the state. The Governor and the State Superintendent of Public Instruction were required to appoint a Textbook Commission of seven members to serve for five years each.   This commission was asked to prepare an outline course of study setting forth what subjects should be taught in each of the elementary grades and the number of basal and supplementary books on each subject to be used in each grade.   The multiple list adopted by the Textbook Commission was submitted to the State Board of Education, which selected from it for adoption two primers for the first grade, two readers for grades one through three, and one basal book for each of the other subjects in the elementary grades.

Provision was made for enforcing this law by granting the State Superintendent of Public Instruction the power to revoke the certificate of any teacher or principal not complying with its requirements.[75]

In 1929 the State Board of Education was ordered to adopt for use in all public high schools a multiple list of high school textbooks based on recommendations of a State Textbook Committee.

---

[73] *Supplement to North Carolina Code*, 1929, Sec. 5440a.
[74] *P. L. of N. C.*, 1919, Chap. 201, Sec. 1–4.   [75] *P. L. of N. C.*, 1921, Chap. 45, Sec. 1–3.

The board was also given the power to fix the number of high school textbooks to be placed in this multiple list.

Evaluation in Terms of the Criteria

The centralizing tendency which has prevailed in matters relating to the public school curriculum has had some influence upon equalization of educational opportunity, as established by the first criterion. Although the several curriculum prescriptions which have been introduced since 1900 have emphasized a certain subject or phase of education, these requirements have not been rigidly enforced and thus have left room for some adaptation by the local communities.

The centralization of the curriculum requirements in the state authorities has made it somewhat difficult to carry out the second criterion—opportunity for local initiative and experimentation in this field.

Matters relating to the *interna* of education include what is taught and how it is taught. The developments which have occurred in the field of the curriculum are, therefore, opposed to the principle established by the criterion relating to *interna* and *externa*.

It is evident that the centralizing tendency relating to the curriculum has not fulfilled the requirements set up in the third criterion, and has worked against the consideration of the educational program as a whole.

TEACHERS' TRAINING, CERTIFICATION, AND SALARIES

The General Assembly of 1901 passed a law requiring that all teachers have certificates. At that time teachers' certificates were issued by county superintendents, by the normal schools of the state, by the teachers colleges, and by the superintendents of special districts. The certificates issued by institutions were declared to become void if the holder failed to teach in the schools of the state for three consecutive years.[76]

The 1905 session provided for county examinations for teachers' certificates and defined the percentages that had to be achieved in order that applicants might qualify for the three different grades of certificates. The act also stated that first-grade certificates would be valid for two years and that the other grades

[76] *P. L. of N. C.*, 1901, Chap. 4, Sec. 22.

would have to be renewed by examination annually.[77]   These regulations did not decrease the number of certificating agencies nor did they standardize the examinations given by the county superintendents.

With the encouragement of the establishment of high schools in 1907 a minimum salary law for certificated high school teachers was passed.   This law helped make possible the opening of many small high schools throughout the state.   Like the other salary laws which had preceded it, it did not determine the amount to be paid to a teacher during any school year, but merely the number of dollars per month to be paid from the state fund:

> . . . The minimum salary of any public high school teacher holding such certificate and employed as high school teacher in such high school shall be forty dollars per school month.[78]

A state certificate was introduced in 1907.   Only those holding first-grade certificates and having successfully completed one year of teaching were eligible to take the examination for the state certificate which was conducted by the county superintendent or some other person selected by the State Board of Examiners. The questions were to be furnished by the board and the papers submitted, examined, and graded by them.   Candidates making a general average of 90 per cent or more received the certificate, which was valid in any county of the state, good for five years, and called for a minimum salary of $35 per month for the holder.[79]

The "State Board of Examiners and Institute Conductors" was established by the 1917 legislature.[80]   This board was granted the power of awarding all first-grade certificates.   The 100 county superintendents and the 136 superintendents of specially chartered districts were still empowered to give out second- and third-grade certificates.   Teachers holding certificates from the former state board of examiners; those holding first-grade county certificates; and those holding certificates from superintendents of specially chartered districts received new state certificates without taking examinations.   Holders of the latter certificates received from the state board state certificates of the grade requested by the superintendent of the specially chartered district from which they had received their certificates.

---

[77] P. L. of N. C., 1905, Chap. 533, Sec. 9.   [78] P. L. of N. C., 1907, Chap. 820, Sec. 4.
[79] P. L. of N. C., 1907, Chap. 835, Sec. 1 (i).   [80] P. L. of N. C., 1917, Chap. 146, Sec. 2.

The types of certificates were increased by the legislature of 1919 to include a superintendent's certificate issued by and under the regulations of the State Board of Examiners.[81] The same session of the legislature increased the salaries of those possessing state certificates from 10 to 25 per cent and the salaries of teachers owning second-grade certificates from $35 per month to $45 per month.[82]

The special session of the General Assembly in 1920 adopted a law directing the State Superintendent of Public Instruction to set up a "uniform graduated salary schedule" for educational employees "based upon training, duties, experience, professional fitness, and continued service in the same school system." This act brought about the basing of salaries on certain definitely stated professional and scholastic requirements, a method which was more equitable than the former method of basing salaries on the grade of certificate held.

> The State Superintendent of Public Instruction shall recommend annually to the State Board of Education for its adoption a uniform graduated salary schedule for all teachers, principals, superintendents, and assistant superintendents, based upon training, duties, experience, professional fitness, and continued service in the same school system, consistent with the estimated amount to be derived from the State Public School Fund . . . nothing in this section shall prevent boards of county commissioners from providing funds sufficient to meet a salary schedule higher than that provided by the State Board of Education. When the State Board of Education shall adopt a graduated salary schedule this shall be the basis for the apportionment of the State Public School Fund.[83]

The effect this new plan for salaries and certifications had on the teachers of North Carolina is expressed by State Superintendent Brooks in the introduction to the 1921 report of the State Educational Commission, in the following terms:

> The special session of the General Assembly of 1920 accepted the proposed salary schedule. At once a demand arose on the part of teachers for further training, and over seven thousand attended summer school in order to raise the grade of the certificate held and command the correspondingly higher salary. Nothing has so stimulated the teaching profession as the Certification-Salary Plan.[84]

The General Assembly of 1921 authorized the creation of a "Division of Certification of Teachers" in the following words:

[81] *P. L. of N. C.*, 1919, Chap. 254, Sec. 5.
[82] *Ibid.*, Chap. 114, Sec. 2.   [83] *P. L. of N. C.*, Special Session, 1920, Chap. 91, Sec. 4.
[84] *Public Education in North Carolina*, p. xi.

There shall be created in the office of the Superintendent of Public Instruction a division of certification of teachers, having a director and such assistants, clerks, and stenographers as may be necessary consistent with the appropriation made for this division. All rules and regulations governing the certification of teachers passed by the State Board of Examiners and Institute Conductors, and now in force, shall be continued in full force and effect until amended or repealed by the authority of the State Board of Education, which is hereby constituted the legal board for certificating or providing for the certification of all teachers after April first, one thousand nine hundred and twenty-one.[85]

The transfer of certification duties from the State Board of Examiners and Institute Conductors to the State Board of Education helped to make the creation of the Division of Certification of Teachers a real step toward the centralization of authority in regard to the qualifications of individuals to teach in North Carolina.

The lack of adequately trained teachers caused the passage of a law by the 1921 Assembly creating a "Division of Teacher Training," made up of a director, not more than four supervisors, and as many assistants as were necessary and as could be paid for out of the annual appropriation of $25,000.[86] At the same time a "Division of Negro Education" was established to have direction of all elementary schools, high schools, teacher-training departments, training schools, and normal schools for Negroes.

The State Board of Education was given control and supervision of the Appalachian Training School and the Cullowhee State Normal and Industrial School as another method of increasing the supply of adequately trained teachers for the public schools of the state.[87]

All the laws passed in 1921 referred to above aided in securing a better teaching staff for the schools of the state. Some of the localities, however, found difficulty in meeting their payrolls, and the following act was put through by the extra session of the General Assembly of 1921 to meet this emergency:

The Treasurer of the State of North Carolina is hereby fully authorized, empowered, and directed, by and with the advice and consent of the Governor and Council of State, to borrow such sum of money, not to exceed seven hundred and ten thousand dollars, as may be required, and at the lowest obtainable rate of interest, not to exceed 6 per cent, to pay any and all of said deficit in the public school fund necessary to meet the salaries of teachers and school

[85] *P. L. of N. C.*, 1921, Chap. 146, Sec. 16.   [86] *Ibid.*, Sec. 15.
[87] *Ibid.*, Chap. 61, Sec. 1.

officials in accordance with the provisions of section five thousand four hundred eighty-two of the Consolidated Statutes. . . .[88]

The next step which concerned the teachers of the state was taken in 1931 when detailed provisions were set up with respect to the number of elementary and high school teachers which each of the administrative units might include in the state budget for the six months' term. The final power of determining the number of teachers was placed in the hands of the State Board of Equalization. In rural areas one teacher was allowed for every thirty-two pupils in average daily attendance in the elementary schools and one teacher for every twenty-seven pupils in average daily attendance in the high schools. Additional teachers for counties not having completed reorganization of districts were allowed at the pleasure of the State Board of Equalization if they considered the reasons for the non-completion to be valid.

The rules and regulations governing the budgets of all the school districts of the state were so strict, as far as the state-supported six months' term was concerned, that the General Assembly appropriated an emergency fund to cover the salaries of teachers who might be needed but whose salaries could not be fitted into the county budgets under the many restrictions and definitions of the items of the budgets.

. . . That the appropriation of one hundred and fifty thousand ($150,000) dollars carried in the Appropriation Act of one thousand nine hundred and thirty-one, where referred to shall be used by the State Board of Equalization as an emergency fund for the salaries of emergency teachers, and allocated to such schools as the said Board of Equalization may determine, and for such other emergencies as may arise, and are not included in the budget of the various counties.[89]

. . . For recently consolidated districts or for new consolidations, the county board of education may request one or more teachers in addition to the number allowed on the basis of the attendance for the next preceding year, but the final determination shall rest with the State Board of Equalization.[90]

Many of the actions taken by the legislators of North Carolina in 1931 were for the purpose of effecting economies. None of the many enactments were more clearly for this reason than the merger of the University of North Carolina, the North Carolina State College of Agriculture and Engineering, and the North

---

[88] *P. L. of N. C.*, Extra Session, 1921, Chap. 8, Sec. 1.
[89] *P. L. of N. C.*, 1931, Chap. 430, Sec. 1 (1931).   [90] *Ibid.*, Sec. 11.

Carolina College for Women into "The University of North Carolina." [91] This is of interest in discussing teacher training and certification because of the courses in education offered by each of the merging institutions. The unified administrative control makes possible the elimination of overlapping courses and the future planning of courses for prospective teachers according to the type of teacher which each institution is best qualified to train. This step, along with the placing of the normal schools under the control of the State Board of Education, did not result in the complete centralization of teacher-training agencies but had the effect of organizing into two administrative bodies the many separate entities which held sway previously.

The system of certification was altered in 1931 by a change in the prerequisites necessary for securing a license to become a county superintendent of schools:

> No person shall be employed as county superintendent of schools unless such person is a graduate of a four-year standard college and has had three years of successful teaching experience or its equivalent, within the ten years next preceding the date of employment, and holds a certificate from the State Board of Education showing these facts: (Provided), that this section shall not apply to persons who now hold a county superintendent's certificate. [92]

While these 1931 professional qualifications were not difficult of fulfillment, they represented an advance over the previous requirements and a basis on which more detailed and specific provisions regarding training and experience could be established. In securing equality of educational opportunity for the children of the state it is just as important to have certain minimum requirements for the position of county superintendent of schools as for the teaching positions which are under his direction and supervision. The mistakes of a poorly trained or immature county superintendent have an almost immediate influence on the schools in the area in which he serves. His responsibilities as a liaison officer between the state officials and the districts under his control are large and of considerable importance.

The School Machinery Act of 1933 caused the State Board of Equalization to be disbanded on May 15, 1933, and a State School Commission to be created in its stead. The powers and duties concerning teachers and salaries formerly vested in the State Board of Equalization were transferred to the new State

[91] *P. L. of N. C.*, 1931, Chap. 202, Sec. 1.   [92] *Ibid.*, Chap. 430, Sec. 19.

School Commission, consisting of the Governor, the Lieutenant Governor, the State Treasurer, and the State Superintendent of Public Instruction, and one member from each congressional district appointed by the Governor. The State School Commission was entrusted with the duty of deciding how many teachers may be included in the state budget for each county and city administrative unit. The determination of the State Standard Salary Schedule for teachers and principals was left to the State Board of Education and to the State School Commission. No teacher or principal could be paid from the State Education Fund supporting the eight months' school term more than the salary specified in the salary schedule adopted by the State Board of Education and the State School Commission. While a school month was defined as consisting of four weeks and not less than twenty teaching days, it was made possible for a local school to increase its six months' term to an eight months' term by increasing its school week from five to six days or by increasing its school day by adding one hour of instructional service to the customary day. Local schools could fabricate this eight months' term only with the approval of the local school authorities and the all-powerful State School Commission, which was also given the right to adjust teachers' salaries when such an "extension" of term took place.

The only change made in the certification laws was to add to the eligibility requirements of the office of county superintendent of schools a doctor's certificate showing the applicant to be free from any contagious disease. However, the elections of the various county boards were made subject to the approval of the State School Commission and the State Superintendent of Public Instruction.

Evaluation in Terms of the Criteria

The creation of the "Division of Certification of Teachers" in 1921, inasmuch as it reduced the number of certificating authorities from over two hundred to one, was a centralizing tendency of primary importance. It helped to carry into effect the principle of equalization of educational opportunity because it insured that teachers unable to measure up to the prescribed minimum requirements would not be certificated. It standardized the requirements for securing the various types of certificates. Since this certificating body was established as a part of the State Department of Education, it is acceptable under the principle of equalization of educational opportunity and equalization of school support.

Ample opportunity is provided for local initiative and experimentation. The requirements established by the state certificating body are minimum in nature and none of the regulations prohibit or discourage the hiring of teachers with higher qualifications. The selection of teachers is also left to the local school district, the only requirement being that they must hold certificates. The status and qualifications of teachers are defined as *externa* in the discussion of the second criterion concerning the relationship of centralization to *externa* and *interna*. Since certification falls under the heading of *externa*, it is considered a desirable field for the exercise of movements toward centralization.

Well-qualified teachers are one of the most important means of maintaining a "well-balanced" educational program. Certification of all teachers under the direction of a central authority helps to bring about higher qualifications for teachers and to provide that all teachers shall have had similar training for the type of position which they hold. Since teachers already employed automatically received certificates when the new regulations were adopted, it follows that new teachers were the only ones affected by this change in policy.

The formation in 1921 of the Division of Negro Education, and the placing of the Appalachian Training School and the Cullowhee State Normal School under the direction of the State Board of Education were steps in the centralization of the higher educational agencies of the state. The merging of the State College of Agriculture and Engineering, the North Carolina College for Women, and the University of North Carolina into the "University of North Carolina" in 1931 was another major move tending to combine the higher educational offerings of the state.

These consolidations followed the principles of equalization of educational opportunity and equalization of school support by making possible the organization of better training courses for prospective teachers, the elimination of overlapping courses, more support from state funds, and in the case of the Division of Negro Education and two normal schools, the direct supervision of the State Department of Education.

State colleges and normal schools are not necessarily local institutions. There is no need for maintaining local initiative or local opportunity for experimentation. These features are neither necessary nor desirable in conducting these colleges and training schools or the state university.

The three unifications which took place had to do with the "qualifications and status" of teachers and as such they are included under the definition of *externa* which is part of the description of the second criterion. They may be considered to be desirable from the standpoint of this criterion.

The needs of the whole program of education are apt to be better taken care of with the mergers which have taken place. They enable the state authorities to deal with three bodies in charge of teacher training and higher education rather than with the ten or twelve lines of authority which existed before.

The power granted the State Board of Equalization in 1931 to determine the number of teachers to be included in the state budget for each locality and later given to the State School Commission with the disbanding of the State Board of Equalization was a severe blow at local initiative. The State Standard Salary Schedule established by the State School Commission and the State Board of Education, accompanied as it was by legislation abolishing all special taxes for school purposes except those needed to pay debts incurred, made it very difficult for any locality to pay teachers more than the salary called for by the state schedule. Voting for a special tax for school purposes in 1934, when the state is supporting a minimum program for eight months, is vastly more difficult than continuing a school tax which may have been established in the years before the current depression when the state was supplying funds but not assuming the whole support.

Equalization of educational opportunity is partly carried out by both of these acts of centralization because provision is made for minimum requirements for a number of teachers and the salaries to be paid to them. The whole principle is not met since the control of the number of teachers and their salaries is placed in the hands of the State School Commission instead of under the State Department of Education.

Little opportunity is provided for local initiative. To be sure, the administrative units may vote a tax for additional school funds, but in times of economic stress communities are not likely to add to their tax burdens. Under the former plan of state aid each community was encouraged to go as far as it wished beyond the minimum program which was partly supported by state contributions. With that method in operation, certain localities conducted schools for nine months and longer and were looked up to as leaders in the public education system of the state. All of the taxes which they had voted to levy annually were swept away by the action of the General Assembly in 1933.

The establishment of certain minima relating to size of classes and number and salaries of teachers pertains to *externa;* therefore, so far as the second criterion is concerned, they are suitable phases of education for centralizing purposes.

State control of the number of teachers and of the maximum salaries, unless a special school tax is voted, hardly insures that every locality will be blessed with the balanced educational program which it desires.   A very poor district, unable or unwilling to vote a special tax, might have need for more teachers than the State School Commission would permit, and for specially trained teachers commanding higher salaries than the state standard salary schedule established.   Such a case could, of course, be appealed to the State School Commission, but there would be little likelihood of favorable action unless the legislator appointed to the Commission from that part of the state could swing the votes of his or her constituents.

SUMMARY

Centralizing tendencies in North Carolina have all been rather closely related to the state support provided for the public schools. This has been due to the fact that state support has been based on taxable values and the cost of maintaining a mimimum school term.   The fact that North Carolina has long experienced difficulty in securing sufficient funds for the support of her school system has tended to focus attention on the system of state support.   While the principle of equalization has been recognized by state apportionments since 1901, North Carolina has now gone to the extremes of complete state support and state control of local budgets and items and objects of expenditure.

This financial power has been centered in a State School Commission rather than in the State Department of Education.   The result of this undue centralization of the financing of the schools in a state body largely political in membership seems to be a virtual denial of opportunity for the functioning of local initiative. Even if the State School Commission were able to bring about a fair degree of equalization of educational opportunity, it is contended that the extreme centralization involved would in the long run operate to interfere with the progress of education in the state.

CHAPTER III

CENTRALIZING TENDENCIES IN THE ADMINISTRATION OF PUBLIC EDUCATION IN MARYLAND

THE Maryland constitution of 1868 provided for the public education of the citizens of the state by general rather than detailed provisions. This has permitted the changing of legal requirements affecting the educational program as the needs and attitudes of the local administrative units have developed. However, even before 1900 tendencies toward a centralizing of certain aspects of educational administration manifested themselves, and in the course of the following discussion those tendencies which had their beginnings prior to the turn of the century will be described from their origin.

STATE SUPPORT

Financial support for a state-wide system of public schools, with funds collected by the state and distributed to the localities, did not assume real importance until 1904 [1] when a state tax of 15 cents on each $100 of taxable property was levied "to pay the salaries of the teachers of the several counties and to provide school books and stationery for the children of the State." [2] This provision for the collection of a state tax and its return to the several counties had its origin in a similar law approved by the 1872 session of the General Assembly. The tax at that time was set at 10 cents on each $100 and the funds were to be used for salaries, stationery, and books. [3] In 1896, $150,000 was appropriated from the state school monies to be used specifically for the purchase of textbooks, [4] while in 1904 the state school tax was allocated for salaries and stationery as well as books.

The 1904 enactment also empowered and required counties in

[1] *Laws of Maryland*, 1904, Chap. 584, Sec. 1 (100). Hereafter referred to in the footnotes of this chapter as *L. of Md.*
[2] *Ibid.*, Chap. 584, Sec. 1 (22).
[3] *Maryland Code*, 1888, Art. 77, Chap. 19.
[4] *L. of Md.*, 1896, Chap. 135, Sec. 2.

which the share of the state school tax was inadequate for salaries, books, and stationery, to levy a tax upon assessable property. This tax was not to exceed 15 cents on the $100 unless the county concerned obtained the approval of the county commissioners.[5] Although the granting of tax monies by the state to the counties started as a general return to the counties of taxes collected by the state to make possible the maintenance of schools and the furnishing of free textbooks to the children attending, it soon came to be based on certain additional specific phases of the educational program which the state desired to encourage. In 1916 state aid was being employed to help finance approved high schools; approved colored industrial schools; the salaries of county superintendents, supervisors, and attendance officers; and the purchase of textbooks, materials of instruction, and school supplies. The state school budget was also required by law to indicate the amount appropriated for teachers' pensions, state normal schools, and the State Department of Education.[6]

The state legislature appropriated $150,000 at the 1918 session for additional compensation to teachers who had received meager salaries for their services during the school year 1917–1918. For white teachers employed for nine months at an annual salary of less than $600, the state offered to pay one-half the difference between their salaries and $600, but not more than $50 to any one teacher. Colored teachers regularly employed for seven months at an annual salary of less than $600 were to be paid one-half the difference between their salaries and $600, but no one of them was to receive more than $25 from the state. The same law requested the counties and the city of Baltimore to match the state payments, but did not obligate them to do so.[7]

The action of the 1918 legislature in voting additional compensation to teachers receiving less than $600 in annual salary was followed by the minimum salary law enacted by the 1920 session. This law provided that no white public school teacher regularly employed should receive less than $600 per school year. It also established higher minimum salaries for white teachers and principals holding certain specified certificates and having had teaching experience of various periods of years.[8]

Financial support for certain parts of the public school program

[5] *L. of Md.*, 1904, Chap. 584, Sec. 1, par. 22.   [6] *L. of Md.*, 1916, Chap. 506, Subchap. 3 (17B).
[7] *L. of Md.*, 1918, Chap. 252, Sec. 1 and 2.   [8] *L. of Md.*, 1920, Chap. 118.

was provided for in 1920 with two acts—one designed to encourage secondary education, the other to foster industrial education for colored children. The high schools receiving state aid were listed in three groups according to the number and average daily attendance of pupils enrolled, the number of teachers employed, and the number of years and quality of instruction given. The promotion of pupils from grade to grade was subject to the approval of the county superintendent of schools, while graduation from high school required the approval of the State Superintendent of Schools. It was also stipulated that state aid would not be granted if the building, equipment, supplies, library, laboratories, or teachers were unsatisfactory to the State Board of Education.[9]

In the administration of state funds the State Board of Education provided for annual inspection of all high schools receiving state aid. Certain restrictions were established limiting the granting of state aid to one high school in each town or city unless each additional high school had an average daily attendance in excess of two hundred pupils, and, in case there were two "white" high schools located in the same city, it was decided that neither should receive more than $2,500.[10]

State aid in 1922 was calculated on the basis of the cost of instruction, with the amount allowed for each teacher and principal dependent upon the "group" to which the high school belonged. The general ruling was made that state aid should not exceed one-half the salary paid to any high school principal or teacher. Public high schools in the city of Baltimore were given $6,000 each as their share of state aid. High schools of the first group were entitled to maximum aid of $5,000; those in the second group, $1,200 as a total grant; and high schools of the third group, the sum of $650.[11]

County boards of education were delegated to establish central colored industrial schools as the need for them became manifest. The special appropriation for this type of school was allotted only if the State Superintendent of Schools or some member of his staff approved the school on visiting it. The $1,500 paid to the treasurer of the county board of the county in which the colored industrial school was started was intended only in part for the new school — one-half of the appropriation was to be used to pay the

[9] *L. of Md.*, 1920, Chap. 118.   [10] *Ibid.*   [11] *L. of Md.*, 1922, Chap. 382.

salary of a colored supervisor who was to visit all the colored schools of the county and help the teachers to make instruction of an industrial character part of the daily program. Payment of this sum was discontinued after the first year unless the colored industrial school had maintained an average attendance of thirty pupils and a minimum of ten colored schools had been conducted in the county concerned. Some discretion was given the State Superintendent of Schools in regard to awarding $750 to counties having a colored industrial school but maintaining less than ten colored schools.[12]

The "Maryland Plan of Equalization" was brought into existence by legislation enacted in 1922. The fact that the Maryland state school system was organized on the basis of the county unit greatly facilitated the application of the equalization principle. Maryland's minimum salary law, based on the grade of certificate possessed, with increments for teaching experience, provided an important stimulus for improving the professional training of the teachers of the state. The equalization fund was created as an appropriation in addition to all the previous state aid quotas.

It was provided that the state should pay the entire school maintenance budget for the minimum state program, less the amount that the county could raise by a 67-cent tax. The number of teachers required for the minimum program was based on the number of pupils in attendance. The further provision that not more than 76 per cent of the county school maintenance budget should be expended for teachers' salaries was added to make sure that sufficient funds would be available to provide adequately for classroom supplies and equipment. This method of financing the public schools of the state was recognized by the National Education Association in 1930 as the best state system for apportioning school funds.[13]

The fact that every county was required to submit a budget showing the cost of providing the minimum school program, and that the State Tax Commission had been working diligently to secure uniform assessments of property values throughout the state, aided in the equalizing power of the legislation passed in 1922.

[12] *L. of Md.*, 1916, Chap. 506; 1920, Chap. 118.
[13] *Research Bulletin of the National Education Association*, Vol. 8, No. 21, p. 86, March, 1930.

The influence of the state on county taxation and expenditures in 1922 may be comprehended from the following quotation from the law:

. . . provided, that the board of county commissioners of each of the several counties sharing in the Equalization Fund shall levy and collect an annual tax for the schools of not less than sixty-seven (67) cents on each one hundred ($100) dollars of assessable property, exclusive of the amount levied for debt service and capital outlay for the schools; provided, further, that in any county all funds which the county board of education may be authorized to expend for the schools, other than State appropriations, and exclusive of the amount authorized to be expended for debt service and capital outlay, may, for the purposes of the above proviso, be considered as levied by the board of county commissioners, irrespective of the source or sources from which such funds may be derived; and provided, further, that the county board of education in each of the several counties sharing in the Equalization Fund shall expend no less than twenty-four per centum (24 %) of the total budget, not including debt service and capital outlay, for purposes other than teachers' salaries. But no special appropriation to any county, except as heretofore in this section provided, or to any academy, or to any college or university may be paid from the General State School Fund.[14]

In 1933 two important changes were made in the law governing the Equalization Fund. The state agreed to increase its distribution of funds to county boards to include monies to enable them to pay the minimum salaries of county superintendents, supervising teachers and helping teachers, high school and elementary school teachers, and teachers in colored schools. It was also determined that payments by the state from the general state school fund would include the cost of transporting pupils to elementary schools and one-half the cost of conveying pupils to high schools when the transportation was approved by the State Superintendent of Schools.

The county commissioners of each county participating in the Equalization Fund were directed to collect a tax of 47 cents on each $100 of real property for expenditures for current expense. Each county receiving support from the state fund was obliged by law to spend at least 24 per cent of the current expense budget, minus costs of transportation, for expenditures other than teachers' salaries.[15]

The advantages to the state of a county unit for educational purposes were seen early in Maryland. The need for a relatively large local unit for purposes of taxation and administration may

[14] L. of Md., 1922, Chap. 382, Sec. 133.   [15] L. of Md., 1933, Chap. 261, Sec. 204.

not have been the primary reason for the creation of the county unit, but regardless of the forces that brought about its establishment the county unit encouraged tendencies toward centralization. There was an element of equalization in the method of collecting funds by means of a state-wide tax and apportioning them according to population among the localities from which they came. It is possible that this early system of financing public education made the introduction of state aid on an equalization basis easier than it would have been had the people been accustomed to deriving a greater proportion of the necessary expenditures from direct local taxation.

Perhaps the most important legislation connected with the distribution of state aid was that concerned with minimum salaries and state-approved high schools. Teachers were protected by this action from the meager salaries which some communities had been paying and, with the increased standards set up, new teachers were required to have had more training. The authority of the State Department of Education to approve and classify high schools, especially in rural areas, improved their educational standards and helped to prevent the organization of high schools with inadequate enrollment and teaching staffs.

From 1922 on, the state's practice of paying the salary of one attendance officer in each county was an important factor in the steady improvement in the enforcement of the compulsory attendance law. Many of the counties might have spent this amount of money for other types of educational service if it had not been earmarked for this particular purpose.

The education of handicapped children received recognition in 1904, when it was provided that deaf children between the ages of eight and sixteen should attend a school for the deaf for eight months or receive instruction equal to public school instruction elsewhere.[16] A similar law was passed in 1906 with regard to blind children. In the same year the deaf and blind children residing in Maryland were aided in securing an education by the state's assumption of the cost of transportation in cases in which the family could not afford to pay these costs.[17] A special fund was set aside in the state school budget in 1931 to assist counties within the state in the education of handicapped children. Each special class for the handicapped is considered as a separate unit

---

[16] L. of Md., 1904, Chap. 299.   [17] L. of Md., 1906, Chap. 236.

in calculating the cost of the minimum program which is the basis for determining the amount of equalization aid to which each county is entitled.[18]

In 1902 provision was made whereby the State Board of Education might retire those who had attained the age of sixty after twenty-five years of service in the public or normal schools of the state. The same act enabled the board to pay a pension of $200 per annum to those it might retire.[19] In 1920 the "pension system" was changed into a "retirement system."[20] Administered by a "retirement board" composed of the State Superintendent of Schools, the State Treasurer, the State Insurance Commissioner, and three members of the retirement association, the act called for contributions by the teachers as well as by the state, the use of McClintock's table of mortality, and the setting up of individual accounts for each member of the retirement association. For each teacher a separate account was established into which the state paid the same amount that the teachers deducted from their salaries. Teachers with twenty-five years of service might, on reaching their sixtieth birthdays, receive a pension of $400 a year if they were unable to teach any longer, were without means of comfortable support, and if they were recommended by the county board and placed on the teachers' retired list by the state superintendent, with this action approved by the State Board of Education. In 1927 the retirement system was placed on an actuarial basis with possible retirement at the age of sixty and compulsory retirement at the age of seventy. A disability allowance was arranged to be based on the salary and years of service of the particular teacher drawing the allowance. Regardless of length of service, it was decided that teachers leaving the system should receive their personal contributions plus 4 per cent interest.[21]

Evaluation in Terms of the Criteria

State aid for public education in the State of Maryland has developed gradually to meet the demands of the program as it has sought to equalize educational opportunity and support throughout the state. It is evident from the preceding discussion that the equalizing power of state aid, both for opportunity and for support, has been great.

---

[18] *L. of Md.*, 1931, Chap. 159.   [19] *L. of Md.*, 1902, Chap. 196, Sec. 1.
[20] *L. of Md.*, 1920, Chap. 447 and 509.   [21] *L. of Md.*, 1927, Chap. 344.

There are many communities with schools which maintain only the standards required by the state, but the fact that others have gone beyond these standards is proof that the minimum standards set up by the state in connection with the policy of state aid have not prevented the functioning of local initiative. Minimum salaries, books, transportation, and aid for high schools may all be classified as *externa*. The monetary aid rendered by the state in organizing colored industrial schools and in supervising the industrial work carried on in the other colored schools may be thought of as affecting one of the *interna*. The extent of the state's influence in this matter is not very great, as there has been little or no attempt to dictate the curriculum or the methods employed in teaching the pupils. Its influence rests in the fact that it has encouraged industrial education by awarding funds to the colored schools for this purpose instead of granting monies to the counties for general educational purposes. We may conclude from the above that state aid in Maryland has concerned itself mainly with matters of *externa* and may therefore be regarded, in general, as favorable from the standpoint of the second criterion.

The monies granted localities by the state help, in general, to support the whole program rather than any special phase of it. The greatest proportion of the funds, to be sure, go to support the minimum salaries required by the State Department of Education. However, the law specifically states that at least 24 per cent of the total current expense budget shall be expended for purposes other than teachers' salaries. This requirement prevents the present method of distribution of state aid from emphasizing the payment of teachers' salaries at the expense of other important items of the budget. State aid in Maryland has seldom helped some types or phases of public education at the expense of the whole program. The funds awarded at various times to buy books, to hire attendance officers, to aid approved high schools, to organize colored industrial schools, or to transport pupils and to pay teachers' salaries have represented in nearly every instance an attempt either to round out the educational offerings or to maintain the program as it had been developed. The chief exception to this policy was the aid offered by the state to encourage the founding of colored industrial schools. The amount of money offered was not large, and one-half of it was designed to be used in hiring a supervisor of industrial work in all the colored schools of the county. There is no evidence that this meager aid caused the educational curriculum for the colored inhabitants to become one-sided or overemphasized in favor of the industrial type of education. There is perhaps no other centralizing tendency that is as widespread and powerful as state aid. The way in which state aid in North Carolina was changed into complete state support is typical of the way in which this centralizing tendency may be made to operate to the detriment of public education, while the above evaluation of the Maryland system of state aid illustrates the benefits which may be derived from a "good" system of state aid.

BUILDINGS

The responsibility for the planning of school buildings was placed in the office of the county school commissioners in 1872 by the following legislative enactment:

. . . every schoolhouse shall be built and furnished according to plans and drawings issued from the office of the county school commissioners.[22]

This law was modified in 1900 to provide that the county school commissioners should "build, repair, and furnish schoolhouses."[23] The rapid increase in school population and attendance, and the increased financial support for public education brought about an increase in building activity. The General Assembly of 1916 recognized the situation by centralizing the responsibility for buildings in the State Department of Education by means of the following law:

The state superintendent shall, subject to the rules and regulations of the state board of education, pass upon all proposals for the purchase of grounds, school sites or buildings, or for the sale of the same, and also upon all plans and specifications for the remodeling of old school buildings or the construction of new school buildings costing three hundred dollars ($300) or more. In case the construction is to be done by the county board itself, it shall be illegal for the county board to proceed until the plans and specifications shall have been approved in writing by the state superintendent of schools; in case the construction is to be done by contract the contract shall be invalid without written approval of the state superintendent of schools.[24]

[22] *L. of Md.*, 1872, Chap. 377.   [23] *L. of Md.*, 1900, Chap. 520, Sec. 1.
[24] *L. of Md.*, 1916, Chap. 506, subchap. 3A, Sec. 20.

The rules and regulations prescribed by the State Board of Education were concerned with the hygienic, sanitary, and protective construction of school buildings and outhouses.

Evaluation in Terms of the Criteria

Before 1872 the erection of buildings for school purposes was left to each locality. The law of 1872 located the authority in the county boards and the act of 1916 shifted the power to the State Department of Education. This centralization aided in the creation of equality of opportunity for it helped to establish certain minimum standards for buildings. It did not emphasize unduly the necessity for adequate, well-planned buildings in empowering the State Superintendent and the State Board of Education to undertake the supervision of the plans for new and altered buildings throughout the state. Local initiative was not discouraged as localities could go beyond the minimum requirements set up by the state board. Although it is true that the lay-out of a building can reduce the effectiveness of an educational program planned with a different arrangement in mind, buildings are one of the *externa* of education, and thus their planning comprises a suitable aspect of education upon which centralizing tendencies may operate. It seems, therefore, from the evaluation of this trend, in the light of the criteria, that it is to be encouraged for the good of the system of public education.

CURRICULUM

Maryland has been active in passing laws concerning the educational curriculum, although the number of subjects in the mandatory list has decreased since the beginning of the century. The following quotation is taken from the 1898 supplement to the Code of Public General Laws of Maryland:

In every district school there shall be taught orthography, reading, writing, English grammar, geography, arithmetic, history of the United States, good behavior, algebra, book-keeping, natural philosophy, the Constitution of the United States, the constitution and history of the State of Maryland, vocal music, drawing, physiology, the laws of health and domestic economy; and the elements of agricultural science may, in the discretion of the State board of education, be added to the branches required to be taught in the State normal school and in the public schools in the various counties of the State. In districts where there is considerable German population, the board of county school commissioners are authorized to cause the German language to be taught, if they think proper to do so.

The list of subjects in 1916 included the following: good behavior, reading, spelling, penmanship, arithmetic, oral and written English, geography, history of the United States and of Maryland, community 'civics, hygiene and sanitation, and such other branches as the State Board of Education might prescribe.[25]

Community civics was required in 1916, while the Constitution of Maryland and the Constitution of the United States were mandatory curriculum materials in 1898. Oral and written English were prescribed in 1916, whereas the corresponding requirement in 1898 was English grammar. Hygiene and sanitation, in the act of 1916, took the place of physiology and laws of health and domestic economy in the 1898 prescriptions. Five subjects, namely, algebra, bookkeeping, drawing, natural philosophy, and vocal music, which were included in the 1898 list of subjects to be taught, were not to be found in the 1916 list.

When the State Board of Education was granted the power to inspect and classify high schools in 1910, another act was passed as follows:

> The State Board of Education shall prepare the course of study to be used by the several groups of high schools described in this Article, and have authority to make any by-law for their government not at variance with the provisions of this Article.[26]

In 1916 this duty was increased in the following manner:

> The State Superintendent of Schools shall prepare, or cause to be prepared, and submit for approval and adoption by the State Board of Education, courses of study for the different grades and kinds of elementary schools, high schools, and normal schools, and also college courses for teachers.[27]

Another subject was added to the prescribed list in 1918 when it was decided that physical education and training should be provided in public elementary and high schools. The enactment carried with it certain minimum time requirements—for elementary schools, fifteen minutes of physical education in each school day and one hour of directed play a week; for high schools one hour of physical education in each school week and two hours of directed play or athletics each week.[28] These time requirements are of particular interest in that they make the mandatory

[25] *L. of Md.*, 1916, Chap. 506, subchap. 7.
[26] *L. of Md.*, 1910, Art. 77, Chap. 386, Sec. 1, subsec. 123B.
[27] *L. of Md.*, 1916, Chap. 506, subchap. 3A, Sec. 20B.
[28] *L. of Md.*, 1918, Chap. 269, Sec. 1.

teaching of the subject more definite and render possible a means of checking upon the carrying out of the law.

Two general tendencies may be seen in this sketch of curriculum prescriptions in Maryland—the first, a tendency to reduce the number of prescribed subjects; the second, a tendency to make the requirements more detailed and specific. These tendencies are diametrically opposed in that the first acts to restore the choice of what shall be taught to the localities, while the second seeks to make more difficult of evasion the will of the state legislature.

Evaluation in Terms of the Criteria

Equality of opportunity does not mean identical opportunities. The enactment of state laws concerning the subjects to be taught interferes with the planning of school programs to meet the needs of localities in which the backgrounds of the pupils or the occupations of the graduates may make desirable a deviation from the program followed in the majority of the communities of the state. The adjustment of the educational offerings to meet individual differences is rendered difficult when there are certain subjects which must be taught whether or not they are of value to the individual concerned.

Local initiative is not entirely disallowed by the state's curriculum provisions as they are minimum rather than maximum requirements. With as many required subjects as there are in Maryland, however, it is difficult to find a place on the schedule for an additional subject if the prescribed course of study is being strictly followed. It is important that local initiative be maintained to encourage those communities that wish to conduct experiments in their programs and offerings, as well as to permit each board of education to adapt its courses to the needs of the boys and girls who attend its schools.

Legislative control of the curriculum affects what is taught in every schoolroom. It may be classed as having to do with the *interna* of education and may be considered an undesirable tendency in the light of this criterion. It is evident that control of the material presented to the children of any large unit of administration, such as a state, is too large a control to place in the hands of a central body too limited in personnel to know at first hand the educational needs of each locality and too often actuated by motives based on political expediency.

The "whole program" is difficult to achieve when certain subjects required by state law must be included even though they may not "belong." Only the more recent legislative acts carry any time provisions, and it is possible to obey the letter of the law by including the required subject in the school day but devoting only a minimum amount of time to its instruction. However, even this plan is time-consuming and interrupts the carrying out of the program which may reasonably be desired.

From the preceding evaluation of this tendency for centralizing the control of the curriculum in the state legislature, it follows that it is undesirable from the standpoint of the criteria set up.

TEACHER TRAINING AND CERTIFICATION

The field of teacher training and teacher certification is one of utmost importance to the efficiency and character of the public school system. Good textbooks, and adequate grounds, buildings, and equipment are of primary importance in the operation of a modern school system—but even the best facilities are wasted, at least partly, when they are at the command of an untrained or immature teacher.

The Maryland Law of 1872 limited the granting of certificates to county examiners and the State Board of Education. Holders of diplomas from the principal of the state normal school were also entitled to be employed as teachers.[29] A state normal school was established in the same year in Baltimore under the control of the State Board of Education which was given the responsibility of appointing the principal.[30] The extent of the board's direction of the state normal school may be found in the following:

The State board of education shall prescribe the course of study and supervise the school in every particular not provided for in this article; they shall make provision for model and experimental primary and grammar schools, under qualified teachers, in which the students of the normal school shall have an opportunity to practice the modes of instruction and discipline inculcated in the normal school. The salaries of the teachers of the model and experimental schools shall be paid in part from the tuition fees derived from the pupils of said model schools.[31]

The number of ways in which a prospective teacher could qualify for a position was increased by an act of the 1904 legislature. Certificates from county superintendents, from the principal of a

---

[29] *Maryland Code*, 1888, Art. 77, Chap. 8, Sec. 48.
[30] *Ibid.*, Art. 77, Chap. 12, Sec. 70. [31] *Ibid.*, Sec. 73.

state normal school of Maryland, from the principal of the normal department of Washington College, and from the State Board of Education were accepted as sufficient evidence on which to employ a teacher. Diplomas from a state normal school of Maryland, from the principal of the normal department of Washington College, or from the normal department of a school or college in Maryland, approved by the State Board of Education; and normal diplomas from other states, approved by the State Superintendent of Public Education, were also considered to qualify individuals for employment as teachers.[32] Applications for life certificates were limited to persons "holding a first-class teacher's certificate, or a diploma of a respectable college, or of a state normal school, who has been a teacher for seven years, of which five shall have been spent in the State of Maryland." [33] The issuing body was the State Board of Education which could annul a certificate for immoral or unprofessional conduct.

The law of 1908 centered the power of approval of degree-granting institutions in the State Board of Education and granted the right to teach to any graduate of a department of pedagogy of a college or university which the board had approved. The diploma received was ordered rated as a first-grade teacher's certificate, subject to classification by the county superintendent of the county employing the holder.[34] This act greatly simplified the issuance and regulation of teachers' certificates by making the State Board of Education the central authority.

The demand for teachers increased rapidly as the school enrollments mounted, and two-year teachers' training courses were authorized in one approved high school of the first group in each county. The necessary regulations and the course itself were to be under the direction of the State Board of Education. It was stipulated that the board should make arrangements to have the diplomas awarded to graduates of the course accepted as certificates to teach in elementary schools.[35] This creation of another means of qualifying for a teaching certificate did not change the situation so far as the centralizing of administration was concerned, as these high school training courses were almost entirely under the control of the State Board of Education.

---

[32] L. of Md., 1904, Chap. 584, Sec. 1, subsec. 48   [33] Ibid., Chap. 584, Sec, 1, subsec. 52.
[34] L. of Md., 1908, Art. 77, Chap. 635, Sec. 1, subsec. 122E.
[35] L. of Md., 1914, Chap. 82, Sec. 1, subsec. 126A.

Many of the teachers already in service were handicapped by insufficient or inadequate professional preparation. In order to overcome this handicap, at least in part, teachers' institutes were ordered to be held in each county once a year. It was decreed that they should be of at least five days' duration and that two or more counties might combine and hold a joint institute. It was further provided that any board of county school commissioners that required at least one-fourth of its teachers to attend a summer school approved by the State Superintendent of Public Education, and that paid at least $25 apiece toward the expenses of the teachers, might dispense with the holding of a teachers' institute for that year. The law required that the county superintendent be given authority to select the teachers to be included in the 25 per cent required to enroll in summer school when this plan was adopted in lieu of holding a teachers' institute.[36]

The General Assembly of 1914 reënacted the main provisions of Paragraph 48, Section 1, Chapter 584, of the Laws of 1904 regarding the various ways in which an individual could qualify for a teaching position. The requirement was added that

. . . after June 1, 1915, no person who has not been previously regularly employed as a teacher shall be appointed a teacher without having had special pedagogic training of at least five weeks in an approved summer school, or its equivalent.[37]

The main reason for adding this prescription seems to have been that some appointments were made by county superintendents of persons having no specific preparation for the teaching profession.

The provision of minimum requirements for the issuing of academic, collegiate, professional, and university degrees, with the placing of authority for drawing up these requirements and for enforcing them in the hands of the State Board of Education, was another tendency toward centralization of the administration of teacher training and certification which occurred at this time. The board was given one year to prescribe the minimum requirements, and educational institutions were allowed one year, after the standards fixed by the board were published, to comply with them. The board was also granted the right to change the requirements from time to time as the changing needs of the state and new standards of education might require.[38]

[36] L. of Md., 1914, Chap. 84, Sec. 1, subsec. 92.   [37] Ibid., Chap. 85, Sec. 1, subsec. 53.
[38] Ibid., Chap. 592, Sec. 1, subsec. 15½.

The state normal schools were placed under the control of the State Board of Education, and all appointments of principals, assistants, and other personnel were to be made by the board.[39] The issuing of teachers' certificates became a function of the State Department of Education after September 13, 1916. The following paragraphs are taken from the legislative enactments which brought this about:

> The state superintendent of schools shall certificate subject to the rules and regulations of the State Board of Education and the provisions of sections 53, 54, and 55 of this article, all teachers in the public schools of this State.[40]
>
> The county superintendent of schools shall be the representative of the state superintendent of schools in all state examinations for teachers' certificates conducted within the county, and shall perform such duties in connection therewith as may be required by the state superintendent of schools.[41]
>
> The state board of education shall prescribe, with and on the advice of the state superintendent of schools, rules and regulations, also the subjects and the standards, subject to the provisions of sections 53, 54, and 55 of this article, for the certification of all the teachers of the State, and for the acceptance of the diplomas of the normal schools, colleges, and universities of Maryland, as well as of other states.[42]

The laws adopted in 1916, governing the professional qualifications in training and experience of county superintendents, assistant superintendents, supervisors, high school principals, elementary school principals, and both regular and special teachers, were greatly strengthened by the minimum salary schedule adopted for county superintendents in the same year,[43] for supervisors and attendance officers in 1918,[44] and for the other positions in 1920.[45]

The policy of aiding in the payment of salaries of qualified persons by means of state funds was begun in 1916 when the state offered to pay one-half of every county superintendent's salary up to $3,000.[46] This practice of state aid for the payment of salaries of certain qualified school officials was expanded, in 1918, to include payment of one-half the salary of a supervisor up to $2,000, and one-half the salary of an approved attendance officer up to $1,200. It was declared that the attendance officer's

[39] *L. of Md.*, 1914, Chap. 124, Sec. 1, subsec. 82.
[40] *L. of Md.*, 1916, Chap. 506, subchap. 3A, Sec. 20A.   [41] *Ibid.*, Sec. 72D.
[42] *Ibid.*, Sec. 1, subchap. 3, par. 12D.   [43] *Ibid.*, Chap. 506.
[44] *L. of Md.*, 1918, Chap. 494.
[45] *L. of Md.*, 1920, Chap. 118.
[46] *L. of Md.*, 1916, Chap. 506.

qualifications should equal those of elementary school teachers holding certificates of the first grade.[47]

The payment of portions of local school officials' salaries by the state was increased in 1922 under the provision that a supervisor might be employed for every forty white elementary teachers and the state would pay two-thirds of the minimum salary. It was also stated that the state would pay the entire salary of one attendance officer ($1,200) in each county and in the city of Baltimore.[48] This same session of the legislature provided for increases in the minimum salaries to be paid qualified teachers, supervisors, and administrators.[49]

The State Board of Education not only developed minimum requirements for certain educational positions but also stipulated the exact nature of the professional training that should be taken. The by-laws of the board provided in 1929 the names and descriptions of courses for those seeking to become high school teachers; the number of observation periods and teaching periods which had to be attended; they further provided that students must rank in the upper four-fifths and make "C" or better in practice teaching to qualify for state certificates; that the head of the department of education must devote full time to the position; periods and teaching periods which had to be attended; that practice teaching must be done in the senior year; that one lesson unit should be taught by the student teacher; that the institution must maintain an adequate library; and other details too numerous to mention.

This centralization of the administration of teacher certification made the prerequisites for entering the teaching profession uniform throughout the state, whereas previously there had been as many standards as there were county superintendents. It allowed prospective teachers the economy and convenience of attending local county examination centers, while it made it necessary for them to measure up to a state-wide standard in order to qualify. The situation affecting persons qualifying by means of educational courses at normal schools, colleges, or universities was unchanged, as the State Board of Education had formerly had authority in regard to which institutions would be approved for the training of teachers for the public schools of the state. Under the new regulations it was much easier for a

[47] *L. of Md.*, 1918, Chap. 494.   [48] *L. of Md.*, 1922, Chap. 382.   [49] *Ibid.*

teacher to move from one county in the state to another in the event that the certificate had been obtained by passing an examination given by a county superintendent. The placing of all certificating authority in the hands of the State Superintendent of Schools was of special importance at this time, owing to the large number of new teachers required to take care of the rapidly increasing enrollment.

The establishment of state normal schools, the power to grant the privilege of conferring degrees, and the right to approve or disapprove degrees from outside the state submitted as credentials for teaching, resulted in the centralizing of the supervision of all teacher-training agencies in the office of the State Superintendent of Schools.

Evaluation in Terms of the Criteria

The centralization of teacher training and teacher certification did a great deal to advance the ideal of equality of educational opportunity. Standardization of requirements for entering the profession and the interpretation of these requirements by one central bureau tended to provide equality of opportunity to the children of Maryland by aiding in the employment of new teachers possessing certain minimum requirements. This tendency did not have as much influence on teachers already in service, since they were not forced to meet the standards. It is true, however, that many of the teachers in service received additional preparation for their work through attendance at summer schools or teachers' institutes.

All the laws which were enacted concerning the training and certification of teachers had to do with teachers in general and not with teachers of a particular subject or course. Since this is true, we may say that the criterion of supporting the whole program of education rather than any specific type or kind was followed.

Matters of training and certification are considered to be *externa* according to the criteria discussed at the end of Chapter I. They are so classified because of the fact that they do not determine what is taught or how it is taught, but by whom the children are taught. Changes in standards of training and certification do not necessarily have any immediate or direct bearing on the actual procedure carried on in the classroom.

Local initiative was not at all interfered with by this placing of the responsibility regarding teacher training and certification in the hands of a larger unit of administration.   Only minimum standards were created and no obstacles were placed in the way of a local community desirous of increasing the standards beyond the minimum set up by the state.

It appears from the application of the criteria that the centralizing tendencies in regard to teacher training and certification help to provide equality of educational opportunity, assist the whole program of education rather than any specific part of it, are concerned with matters having to do with the *externa* of the school situation, and allow opportunity for local initiative.

SUMMARY

Centralization of the administration of the Maryland state school system has come about largely by means of supervision rather than by means of administrative control.   The fact that the county unit was already in use in 1900 aided greatly in setting up the "Maryland Plan of Equalization" in 1922.

The State Board of Education in Maryland has adopted by-laws from time to time which have been just as powerful influences for centralization as legislative enactments.   State Superintendent Cook, who has directed the development of Maryland's system of public schools since 1920, states his opinion of the desirability of educational leadership in the State Department of Education as follows:

The weakness of the American system of education in my judgment is in giving too little opportunity for initiative at the top with too much opportunity for initiative at the bottom, almost entirely unexercised, as in case of our weak district and township unit systems.[50]

[50] Cook, Albert S., "Centralizing Tendencies in Educational Administration." *Educational Administration and Supervision*, Vol. IV, pp. 133–40, March, 1918.

CHAPTER IV

CENTRALIZING TENDENCIES IN
THE ADMINISTRATION OF PUBLIC EDUCATION
IN NEW YORK

THE obligation of the state to support a system of free public schools was not recognized in the constitution of the State of New York until the beginning of 1895. The New York State constitution, adopted on November 6, 1894, and effective January 1, 1895, contained this statement regarding public education:

> The legislature shall provide for the maintenance and support of a system of free common schools wherein all the children of this State may be educated.[1]

While many other states had incorporated the principle of free schooling into their constitutions prior to 1895, some of them had written the provisions in such detailed fashion as to handicap seriously the future development and organization of a state-wide system of public education. New York's constitutional provision was to prove almost ideal in that it provided the state with the necessary powers and left to the legislature the methods and organizations to be employed in carrying them out. Although slow to write public education into its constitution, New York had maintained free schools since 1867 when the so-called rate-bills of 1814 were abolished.[2] These rate-bills legalized the collection of money from parents on the basis of the number of days of instruction their children had received and the amount of the cost of education unpaid after the state apportionment, the town tax, and the district tax had been spent.[3]

Fairlie, in his study of New York State, summarized the developments leading toward centralization in the nineteenth century in the following words:

> . . . the development toward central control in the first half of the century was not without reactionary steps. The office of State Superintendent of

[1] *New York State Constitution*, 1895, Art. IX, Sec. 1.
[2] *Laws of New York*, 1867, Chap. 406. Referred to hereafter in the footnotes of this chapter as *L. of N. Y.*
[3] *L. of N. Y.*, 1814, Chap. 192.

Schools, created in 1812, was abolished in 1821, and the powers of that officer conferred on another official busied with other and unrelated duties. The county superintendent system of supervision, established in 1841, was abandoned after six years' experience. Nevertheless, even in this period, there were permanent measures in the direction of increasing the central authority, prominent among these being the appellate jurisdiction of the State Superintendent, conferred in 1822, and the provision for a Deputy Superintendent in 1841. Since the creation of a separate Department of Public Instruction in 1854, the movement has been uniformly, but not always steadily, in the direction of strengthening the authority of that department. The system of district commissioners, established in 1856, made possible a closer supervision of the local schools; in the legislation of 1864–67 the State Superintendent's control was increased through the supervision of training teachers, and in other details; during the last ten years the entire system of examining teachers has been placed under his immediate direction, and the supervision of school attendance and other details of school management have come to a greater or less degree under his general oversight. The present stage of central control has been reached not by any sudden change of policy, but through a series of measures extending over a period of a hundred years.[4]

The beginning of the twentieth century found New York with a dual system of education. The Board of Regents, which had been incorporated in 1784, still had administrative control over academies and colleges, while the State Superintendent of Public Instruction directed the destinies of the common schools which had come under his administration with the creation of the Department of Public Instruction in 1854. The Department of Public Instruction continued the work begun under the State Superintendent of Common Schools, a position which was established in 1812, and which first brought into being the dual system[5] which continued until the Unification Act of 1904.

STATE SUPPORT

Several grants for special purposes were in effect in the year 1900. Academies and colleges under control of the Board of Regents received annually $250 each for books and apparatus, provided they each spent at least the same amount.[6] Each city of the state, each incorporated village having a population of 5,000 or more, and each union free school district having a population of 5,000 or more and employing a superintendent of schools, received $800 and, in case a city was entitled to more than one member of the Legislature Assembly, $500 for each additional

[4] Fairlie, John A., *The Centralization of Administration in New York State*, pp. 32–33.
[5] *L. of N. Y.*, 1784, Chap. 51; 1854, Chap. 97; 1812, Chap. 242. [6] *L. of N. Y.*, 1834, Chap. 140.

member.[7] This grant was called a "supervision quota." A "district quota," identical with grants later termed "teachers' quotas," was established in 1890 to pay to every school district and city conducting schools for thirty-two weeks $100 for each qualified teacher employed. This quota was still in force in 1900.[8] The funds remaining for common schools after the $800, $500, and $100 grants, or quotas, had been apportioned were distributed to the counties according to their population. Teacher training was carried on by academies and by academic departments of union schools, both of which received financial support for this work from the Board of Regents.[9] The first normal school was founded in 1844 under the joint supervision of the Regents and the Superintendent of Common Schools. Additional normal schools were established in 1848, 1863, 1867, 1885, 1887, 1889, and 1893, so that by 1900 there were twelve institutions devoted to the training of teachers, as well as the academies and high schools which had first received special legislative appropriations in 1834 and 1887, respectively.[10]

The preceding description of the special grants or quotas existing in 1900 has been given to show the beginnings of the quota method of apportionment of school funds which was increasingly utilized up to 1925. While the use of these special quotas may be termed a necessary evolutionary method or device for allocating monies, it may be well to call attention to the fact that the individual quotas bore little relation to one another and that no system or general principle was followed in their creation by the legislature. The primary factor behind each new quota seems to have been the awarding of increased financial aid from the state.

The amount appropriated to schools of academic grade was increased from $106,000 to $350,000 by the legislative session of 1901, which also ordered that the funds be distributed by means of a quota of $100 to each academic school; that a grant equal to the amount raised from local sources, but not more than $250, be made to buy approved books and apparatus; and that the balance be distributed on the basis of the attendance of academic students according to university ordinances.[11]

[7] L. of N. Y., 1889, Chaps. 90 and 333.   [8] L. of N. Y., 1890, Chap. 534.
[9] L. of N. Y., 1887, Chap. 709; 1889, Chap. 529.
[10] L. of N. Y., 1834, Chap. 241; 1848, Chap. 318; 1863, Chap. 418; 1867, Chaps. 6, 21, 195, 199, 223; 1885, Chap. 287; 1887, Chaps. 374, 709; 1889, Chap. 517; 1893, Chap. 553.
[11] L. of N. Y., 1901, Vol. 2, Chap. 498. Sec. 1.

The principles of need and effort based on the number of persons dwelling within the school district, the number of school children, and the number of teachers employed had been recognized in the process of apportioning school appropriations up to 1902. The "district quota" providing $150 for each district having an assessed valuation of $40,000 or less and $125 for the remaining districts and cities of the state was the first recognition in the state's financing of the principle of "ability to pay." [12] The same law required that, after the supervision quotas, the district quota, and the teachers' quota [13] had been allotted, the remainder be divided among the several counties according to their respective populations. This indicated that the principle of "ability to pay" was still to be fully developed as a basis for allotting state support for public education.

In 1902 the academies, as well as the colleges, were still under the supervision of the Regents, while the common schools were under the direction of the State Superintendent of Public Instruction and the Department of Public Instruction. An act was passed at this time permitting the board of education of a union free school district to adopt an academy as an academic department, contract for the instruction of its academic pupils by the academy, and receive the state school money appropriated for the support of academic departments.[14] One year later, in 1903, the state appropriated $100,000 to pay the tuition of non-resident pupils from schools with no academic departments admitted to schools having academic departments. The schools with academic departments accepting non-resident students, in order to qualify for the $20 per year per pupil, stipulated in the act, had to maintain a course of study approved by the State Superintendent of Public Instruction and the Chancellor of the University of the State of New York, operate schools for a minimum of thirty-two weeks in the year, and accept the $20 as full payment for the tuition. Proportionate amounts were allowed for shorter periods of attendance than the thirty-two weeks' minimum, provided they were not less than eight weeks.[15] This action by the legislature helped to provide equal opportunity for

[12] L. of N. Y., 1902, Vol. 2, Chap. 593, Sec. 1.

[13] Formerly called "district quota," and providing to each district or city $100 for each qualified teacher employed. It was designated teachers' quota by act of 1902 and amended to read for each additional teacher $100 and for each Indian reservation for each teacher employed $100.

[14] L. of N. Y., 1902, Vol. 1, Chap. 325, Sec. 1.   [15] L. of N. Y., 1903, Vol. 2, Chap. 542, Sec. 1.

those wishing to attend high school. The provisions of the Act were extended in 1904 when $200,000 was voted the Department of Public Instruction to continue payments of the tuition of children living in areas not having academic departments.[16]

The "Unification Act" of 1904 brought together under the office of State Commissioner of Education the powers and duties formerly divided between the superintendent of public instruction, as the head of the Department of Public Instruction, and the office of the secretary of the Board of Regents. The Commissioner was granted the supervision of elementary and secondary schools, and, as executive officer of the Board of Regents, authority over colleges, technical and professional schools, and universities. Power was also vested in the Commissioner to create departments, appoint deputies and heads of departments, and determine salaries.[17]

State aid for general industrial and trade schools was first introduced in 1908 when $500 was given to each city and union free school district for each independently organized industrial or trade school maintained for forty weeks, employing at least one full-time teacher, having a minimum enrollment of twenty-five pupils and a course of study approved by the Commissioner of Education. Cities or districts employing more than one teacher for this purpose were granted $200 for each additional teacher. Pro-rata amounts were allowed for approved schools operating for less than forty weeks. Seven thousand dollars was appropriated to the educational department to be used in this manner.[18]

The teacher training quota, introduced in 1909, provided that each academy and union free school district conducting a training class with a minimum of ten scholars for a minimum term of thirty-six weeks according to rules and regulations prescribed by the Commissioner should recieve $700. It was further enacted that the Commissioner might allow a term shorter than the minimum or a registration of fewer than ten pupils and allot a proportionate amount of money. Any funds left over after the apportionment described above were to be divided among the cities of the state maintaining training schools, on the basis of the aggregate attendance of the pupils enrolled in each such school.[19]

[16] L. of N. Y., 1904, Vol. 2, Chap. 729, Sec. 1.   [17] Ibid., Vol. 1, Chap. 40, Sec. 4.
[18] L. of N. Y., 1908, Vol. 1, Chap. 263, Secs. 4 and 6.
[19] L. af N. Y., 1909, Chap. 406, Secs. 462 and 641.

Changes in the district quotas which were made the same year tended to help the poorer districts more than had been customary in the past. Those with assessed valuations of $20,000 or less were granted $200; districts with assessed valuations of more than $20,000 but not more than $40,000 were allotted $175; areas for school purposes possessing assessed valuations of $60,000 or less, but more than $40,000, were entitled to $150; each Indian reservation was apportioned $150 for each teacher employed for thirty-two weeks or more; and each remaining district and each one of the cities of the state was to be allowed $125.[20]

The state assumed a new financial relationship to the localities within its borders when the "State Teachers' Retirement Fund for Public School Teachers" was created in 1911. While this was not the first time that the state had enacted legislation concerning the pensioning of its teachers, it was the first time that a fund had been established on a state-wide basis to consist of contributions by both the teachers and the state, the income of which was to be derived from the investment of the monies collected.[21]

The general industrial and trade schools which were first given state aid in 1908 were granted increased aid in 1913 when general industrial and trade schools, schools of agriculture, mechanic arts, and homemaking, and part-time and continuation schools, open to those over fourteen years of age and having a minimum staff of one full-time teacher, a minimum term of thirty-six weeks, and a minimum enrollment of fifteen pupils, were apportioned two-thirds of the salary paid the first teacher, up to $1,000, and one-third of the salary paid for each additional teacher employed, up to $1,000.[22]

A new law in 1914 authorized the Commissioner of Education to lay out districts for the setting up of central schools to teach the courses commonly found in common schools and high schools, including the subject of agriculture.[23] Provision was made for the granting of state aid for central rural districts organized pursuant to the law, in the following words:

Any district organized under the provisions of this act shall from the time of its organization receive from the State the amount of money on the basis of attendance paid to the common school districts included therein during the year

[20] L. of N. Y., 1909, Chap. 21, Art. 17, Sec. 451.
[21] L. of N. Y., 1911, Vol. 2, Chap. 449, Art. 43-B, Sec. 1101.
[22] L. of N. Y., 1913, Vol. 3, Chap. 747, Sec. 1.   [23] L. of N. Y., 1914, Vol. 1, Chap. 55, Sec. 1.

preceding its organization, at the rate that the said districts were then entitled to receive moneys pursuant to law. If a common school district be divided in the formation of a central district the moneys of such common school district shall be apportioned by the commissioner of education, and the share thereof apportioned to that part of the common school district included in the central district shall be paid to the central district. Whenever any such district shall comply with the requirements of section six hundred and four of the education law in relation to the establishment of general schools of agriculture and home-making, the commissioner of education shall make the same annual apportionment of State school moneys to such central school as is now required to be made by law to a high school or union free school district complying therewith. Any such central district shall also receive all other allowances of public moneys apportioned by the State which it would be entitled to receive if it were a union free school district.[24]

This law was the beginning of a movement to bring about the formation of larger school districts in rural areas by merging existing districts.

The public school system of New York State was expanded in 1915 to include "farm schools" to be established in any county outside the City of New York upon a majority vote of the board of supervisors. The purpose of these schools was the giving of instruction in the trades and in industrial, agricultural, and home-making subjects to children from eight to eighteen years of age. Each "farm school" having a minimum term of thirty-six weeks, a minimum enrollment of fifteen pupils, and an organization and course of study approved by the Commissioner of Education, was to receive $1,000 annually and, in addition, $200 per year for each full-time teacher employed.[25] Although these schools were included in the public school system, they were not free. The parents or guardians were to pay the expense of attendance whenever they could do so.

When instruction in physical training was added to the curriculum prescriptions of the state in 1916, state aid for teachers employed for this purpose, amounting to one-half the salary paid each teacher up to maximum aid of $600 for a single teacher, was written into the act.[26]

The Federal Board for Vocational Education was created and organized in 1917. New York accepted the act with its matching provisions in the same year and designated the Board of Regents as the State Board for Vocational Education and the State

[24] L. of N. Y., 1914, Vol. 1, Chap. 55, Sec. 1, par. 185.
[25] L. of N. Y., 1915, Vol. 2, Chap. 307, Sec. 1.   [26] L. of N. Y., 1916, Vol. 3, Chap. 567, Sec. 1.

Treasurer as the custodian of monies to be paid to the state by the Federal Government for the support of vocational education.[27] Both the addition of the subject of physical training to the curriculum and the creation of the Federal Board for Vocational Education were actions influenced by the fact that a World War was raging in Europe.

Central high school districts, to be formed by two or more adjoining school districts for the purpose of offering secondary education opportunities to the children residing in the districts coöperating, were made possible by the 1917 legislature. It was decided that state aid would be apportioned to these districts under the same conditions and regulations as those governing the allotment of funds to union free school districts for secondary instruction given by them. This was another measure seeking to encourage the creation of larger units for school attendance and administration.[28] Another law passed in the same year, concerning classes for physically defective children, stipulated that a board of education having fewer than ten such children might contract with the board of education of another city or school district for their instruction.[29]

Increased support for the teaching of agriculture was brought about by apportioning one-half the salary paid to directors of agriculture up to a maximum of $600 for any one director.[30] New powers in regard to the expenditures of the larger districts of the state were placed in the hands of the Commissioner of Education by the following addition to the Education Law relating to the examination of accounts:

. . . He [the state comptroller] may also upon the request or with the consent of the commissioner of education, cause like inspections and examinations to be made by such examiners so appointed, of the accounts of the school authorities or the school officers of a city or union free school district, having a population of five thousand or more. Whenever an examination is made of the accounts of the school authorities or school officers of a city or of a union free school district, the comptroller shall transmit to and file with the fiscal officer or clerk of the school authorities of the city or school district examined and with the commissioner of education copies of the report of the examination.[31]

There is nothing in the law to indicate what line of action the Commissioner of Education might follow if dissatisfied with the way in which the school accounts were being kept.

[27] L. of N. Y., 1917, Vol. 2, Chap. 576, Sec. 1.   [28] Ibid., Vol. 1, Chap. 137, Sec. 1.
[29] Ibid., Vol. 2, Chap. 559, Sec. 1.   [30] Ibid., Chap. 560, Sec. 1.   [31] Ibid., Chap. 307, Sec. 1.

The sum of $20,000 was appropriated in 1918 for use by the Commissioner of Education in organizing and operating courses of study on methods of instruction of illiterates, at training institutes and state normal schools.[32] In the same session the legislature appropriated $60,000 for the supervision and training of teachers of physical education.[33]

The $20,000 appropriation in 1918 for the instruction of teachers of illiterates was increased in 1919 to $100,000 and was amended to include non-English-speaking persons.[34] The same year saw an increase in the state tuition for non-resident academic pupils from the $20 formerly paid to a new rate of $40 per pupil per year.[35] State scholarships for soldiers, sailors, and marines honorably discharged, providing $100 a year for tuition at any college, university, or normal, technical or trade school in New York State and $100 per year for maintenance, were also created in 1919, and $30,000 was appropriated for this purpose.[36]

A new quota was introduced to pay the expenses of teachers required to attend an institute or conference held outside their local districts.   It was arranged that teachers should receive one dollar for each day or part of a day spent in attendance and ten cents a mile for traveling costs.   This quota was to be paid to the teachers by the district to which they belonged and the districts were to be repaid by the Commissioner of Education any monies expended in this manner.[37]

Salary schedules for members of the supervising and teaching staffs in city schools were set up by the 1919 legislature, which ordered the board of education of each city in the state to adopt by-laws establishing schedules specifying salaries and increments not less than those set up by law for the various population groups into which the cities were divided.   At the same time, in order to help provide the funds with which to pay the salaries, it was enacted that $100 should be apportioned for each teacher employed in a city, common, or union free school district.   While boards of education outside of cities were not forced to adopt salary schedules, it was stipulated that they should increase the salary of each teacher employed at least $100, beginning August 1, 1919.   To make possible this contribution of $100 for each teacher

[32] L. of N. Y., 1918, Vol. 2, Chap. 412, Sec. 1.   [33] Ibid., Chap. 442, Sec. 2.
[34] L. of N. Y., 1919, Vol. 2. Chap. 617, Sec. 1 and 2.   [35] Ibid., Chap. 368, Sec. 1.
[36] Ibid., Chap. 606, Sec. 1 and 2.   [37] Ibid., Vol. 1, Chap. 109, Sec. 1.

employed, \$5,300,000 was appropriated by the state.[38] This step was one of the most important taken during the first two decades of the present century, from the standpoint of the amount of increased state aid involved and the power placed in the hands of the Commissioner of Education over the salaries paid teachers by the cities of the state.

The amount of money distributed by the state to assist in the payment of teachers' salaries was increased in 1920 by an amendment to Section 491-a of the Education Law, carrying a schedule of the amount to be paid by the state for each teacher employed by districts of varying populations. The schedule varied all the way from \$600 per teacher to be paid to cities of the first class with populations of more than a million, to \$200 per teacher to be granted school districts employing only one teacher. The relative wealth of one-teacher districts was taken into consideration by providing that one-teacher districts having an assessed valuation of \$100,000 or less should receive, in addition to the \$200, two dollars for each entire \$1,000 the assessed valuation fell below \$100,000.[39] The amount and method of apportionment of the academic quota were also changed to provide increased state funds and recognition of the number of teachers employed. To cover the cost of these two increased quotas and a 20 per cent bonus to teachers employed in the State Department, there was appropriated \$20,500,000.[40]

Twenty-five industrial teachers scholarships of not more than \$2,000 each were established under the rules and regulations of the Board of Regents in 1920 to meet the need for teachers in vocational schools. The Commissioner of Education was given the pleasure of awarding these scholarships annually, and the winners were to use them for maintenance and support while attending the vocational department of one or more of the state's normal schools. Applicants had to have at least five years of successful experience in trade, industry, or technical occupations to qualify.[41] An "Advisory Commission for the Rehabilitation of Physically Handicapped Persons" was created during the same year, and one of its many duties was to organize special courses in the public schools for the training of the physically handi-

---

[38] *L. of N. Y.*, 1919, Vol. 2, Chap. 645, Sec. 1, 2 and 3.
[39] *L. of N. Y.*, 1920, Vol. 3, Chap. 680, Sec. 2.   [40] *Ibid.*, Sec. 6, 7 and 8.
[41] *Ibid.*, Chap. 853, Sec. 1.

capped. This commission, its membership and duties, are discussed in another part of this chapter under the heading, "The University of the State of New York." [42]

The financial outlays of certain districts for permanent improvements were restricted by the enactment of the following law by the 1920 legislature:

> . . . In districts having an aggregate valuation of real property of one million dollars or over, no bonds shall be hereafter issued which make the total bonded indebtedness, at any time, exceed 10 per centum of the aggregate assessed valuation of the real property within the bounds of such school district.[43]

This law was amended one year later to include districts having an aggregate valuation of $500,000 or over, and the limit of bonded indebtedness was increased to 15 per cent with the added proviso that bonds might be sold in excess of that amount if the authorizing resolution was adopted by two-thirds vote of the qualified electors present and voting at a meeting called to consider this proposition.[44]

The quota granted union free school districts with academic departments was increased from $300 per teacher to $350 per teacher in 1921 and districts employing more than one teacher were allotted $300 per teacher instead of the $250 formerly awarded. One-teacher districts having an assessed valuation of $100,000 or less were given three dollars for each $1,000 the assessed valuation was less than $100,000, whereas they had previously been given only two dollars for each $1,000.[45] Boards of education establishing courses of instruction for foreign born and native adults and minors over sixteen years of age were apportioned one-half the salary paid to teachers of such courses up to $1,000 for each teacher. This financial aid was to be distributed by the state in the same manner as teachers' quotas.[46]

Districts establishing one or more special classes for the instruction of children three or more years retarded in mental development and employing one or more qualified teachers to conduct said classes were entitled by an act of 1923 to receive one-half the salary paid to each teacher up to a maximum of $1,000 for any one teacher. The monies were ordered to be apportioned in the same way that teachers' quotas had been.[47]

[42] L. of N. Y., 1920, Vol. 3, Chap. 760, Sec. 1.
[44] L. of N. Y., 1921, Vol. 2, Chap. 318, Sec. 1.
[46] Ibid., Vol. 2, Chap. 327, Sec. 1.

[43] Ibid., Vol. 1, Chap. 162, Sec. 1.
[45] Ibid., Vol. 3, Chap. 584, Sec. 1.
[47] L. of N. Y., 1923, Chap. 395, Sec. 1.

Financial aid to consolidated districts was apportioned on the basis of the assessed valuation and the number of teaching positions at the time of the consolidation, for all districts formed by consolidation since March 25, 1913. The money so apportioned could be used for the payment of teachers' salaries, the transportation of pupils, and the maintenance of a school or schools. It was also provided that consolidated districts should receive the same amount of state aid for attendance of pupils residing in districts consolidated with a union free school district at a high school or academic department maintained in such union free school district as they would if consolidation had not taken place.[48]

The state system of pensions for teachers assumed new duties and responsibilities in 1923 when the local teachers' retirement and pension systems of every city having a population of less than one million were merged with the state teachers' retirement system. It was arranged that retired persons should receive the same allowances as were given before the merger and that all local contributions should be refunded to those who had not reached retirement age. The State Treasurer was named treasurer for the funds of the dissolved systems.[49] Additional state support for training classes conducted by academies and union free school districts was provided in 1923 through the increase of the training class quota from $700, which it had been since 1909, to $1,200.[50]

Boards of education establishing one or more classes for the instruction of physically defective children and employing one or more qualified teachers to conduct such classes were allowed one-half the salary paid to each teacher up to a maximum of $1,000 for each, by a law enacted by the 1924 legislature.[51] The same session of the legislature provided that the Commissioner of Education should apportion one-half the salary paid, up to a total of $1,000, for medical inspectors, and one-half the salary paid school nurses, health teachers, or health experts, up to $700 maximum apportionment for any single nurse, health teacher, or expert. It was required that each individual should have the qualifications prescribed by the Commissioner of Education, and that their actual employment should be approved by him.[52] School hygiene districts were permitted, and in case the board of supervisors of any county, with the approval of the Commissioner

[48] L. of N. Y., 1923, Vol. 2, Chap. 716, Sec. 1.   [49] Ibid., Chap. 161, Sec. 1.
[50] Ibid., Chap. 162, Sec. 1.   [51] L. of N. Y., 1924, Chap. 193, Sec. 1.   [52] Ibid., Chap. 265, Sec. 1.

of Education, established such a district, it was agreed that the Commissioner would pay one-half the salary and expenses of the district director of school hygiene appointed.[53]

The teacher-training-class quota which had been increased to $1,200 in 1923 was further increased to $2,000 in 1925 with the new provision that any teacher of such a class must be paid a minimum salary of $1,800 a year. It was also enacted that this quota would be granted to a maximum of one hundred such classes during one year.[54] State aid for central rural schools, first introduced in 1914, was increased by the addition of the transportation quota and the building quota in 1925. These two quotas were apportioned only if the total of all expenditures of the district exceeded a sum equal to the amount raised by a five-mill tax on each dollar of assessed valuation of taxable property. The transportation quota consisted of one-half the sum paid for the transportation of pupils when the expenditure was approved by the Commissioner of Education. The building quota was one-fourth the sum spent for the erection, enlargement, or remodeling of a school building in a central rural district and was paid only if the Commissioner of Education had approved the plans and specifications in advance of the outlay of funds for this purpose.[55] The transportation quota was also awarded to other districts besides the central rural districts, as the following quotation illustrates:

There shall also be apportioned and paid to each district created by the consolidation of districts as provided in sections 128, 129 and 132 of this chapter, and under similar provisions of law in force prior to the enactment of this chapter, and to each union free school district, a quota to be known as the transportation quota, equivalent to one-half of the sum paid for the transportation of pupils. Such transportation quota shall only be apportioned and paid where the district shall have voted to furnish such transportation as provided by law, or where the commissioner of education shall direct that such transportation be furnished. Such quota shall not be paid in a case where the provision made for transportation is inadequate and is disapproved by the commissioner of education.

It was further stated that the expenditures, exclusive of public monies, during the year for which the quota was apportioned must be greater than the amount that a five-mill tax on each dollar of assessed valuation of taxable property would raise.[56]

[53] *L. of N. Y.*, 1924, Chap. 194, Sec. 1. [54] *L. of N. Y.*, 1925, Chap. 152, Sec. 1.
[55] *Ibid.*, Chap. 673, Sec. 2. [56] *Ibid.*, Chap. 674, Sec. 1.

The famous "Cole Law" was also enacted in 1925. The major contribution which this law made to New York's system of state aid consisted of the "equalization quotas." These quotas were established in addition to all other existing quotas, for the double purpose of providing increased state support and introducing the principle of equalization. They were payable to each city and other school district maintaining an approved high school or academic department and to school districts not maintaining an academic department or high school which employed five or more elementary teachers and provided adequately for the academic education of children completing the elementary grades. The two main factors involved in the determination of the amounts of these quotas were the value of the taxable property contained in the school districts and the number of teachers employed. Apportionments under these quotas were based on the number of elementary and academic teaching units, with the elementary school unit twenty-seven weighted pupils per teacher and the high school unit twenty-two weighted pupils. The amount allotted under the equalization quota was not to be greater than the amount of the excess of the total expenditures for school purposes when compared with the amount raised by a five-mill tax on the assessed valuation of taxable property plus the public monies accepted by the district. There was set $1,200 as the amount to be distributed for each elementary teaching unit and $1,600 as the amount to be paid for each high school teaching unit, less $1.50 for each $1,000 of actual assessed valuation of taxable property contained in the district. The 1925 legislature also increased the additional teachers' quotas to a minimum of $800 for a school year of forty weeks.[57]

The "equalization quotas" were added to the various quotas which central rural districts were already entitled to receive, by an amendment to the school laws passed by the 1926 session of the legislature.[58] The same session increased the state tuition for non-resident academic pupils from the rate of $40 per pupil per year that had been paid since 1919 to a new rate of $50 per pupil per year that is still being apportioned. Two additions were made to the law, which are explained thus:

City and union free school districts shall not refuse to receive non-resident academic pupils for instruction without valid and sufficient reasons therefor.

[57] L. of N. Y., 1925, Chap. 675, Sec. 1, 491a and 491b. [58] L. of N. Y., 1926, Chap. 299, Sec. 1.

All acts of the board of education or other district officers relating to such pupils and the tuition charged for their instruction are hereby declared subject to review by the commissioner of education.   Where a district is so situated that its academic pupils can be more conveniently instructed in the academic department of a school located in another state, the commissioner of education is hereby authorized to make the same apportionment to such district annually, to be applied in payment of the tuition of each such academic pupil so instructed outside the state, as he shall be authorized by law to make for the instruction of academic pupils within the state, and upon the same conditions.[59]

The 1926 legislature also increased two of the additional teachers' quotas.   The quota applying to school districts other than city and union free school districts employing more than one teacher was increased from $450 to $500 and the quota for common school districts hiring only one teacher and having an assessed valuation of more than $100,000 was made $300 instead of $250, as had formerly been allotted.[60]   State aid for the instruction of physically handicapped children, which was inaugurated in 1924 by an act providing that the state pay one-half the salary up to $1,000 paid to teachers of physically defective children, was increased in 1926 by the assumption by the state of one-half the cost of education and surgical treatment given such children.   The county treasurers were paid one-half the sum expended by the Comptroller of the state, who issued his warrant after receiving certified statements from the Commissioner of Education and the Commissioner of Health.[61]

The additional teachers' quotas were changed in 1927 so that union free school districts maintaining academic departments and other districts having five or more teachers were apportioned $500.   Districts having more than one teacher and fewer than five teachers were granted four $50 increases in four successive years, which made the total quota for each year as follows: $550 for the year beginning August 1, 1927; $600 for the year beginning August 1, 1928; $650 for the year beginning August 1, 1929; and $700 for each year thereafter.   Quotas for one-teacher districts having assessed valuations of $100,000 or less were modified so that none of them should receive less than $300, and the greatest amount of aid would be granted to those one-teacher districts having the smallest assessed valuations.[62]   Each district superintendent received an annual salary from the state, beginning in

---

59 *L. of N. Y.*, 1926, Chap. 752, Sec. 2.   60 *L. of N. Y.*, Chap. 751, Sec. 1.
61 *Ibid.*, Chap. 817, Sec. 3.   62 *L. of N. Y.*, 1927, Chap. 572, Sec. 1.

1917. This salary was increased from $2,400 to $3,000 by an act of 1927, and the requirements for the position were increased to that of college or normal school graduation, three years' experience in teaching or supervision, and the passing of an examination on the teaching and supervision of courses in agriculture.[63]

The "Cole Law" was amended in 1927 to provide for a series of increases to the allotments for elementary and high school teacher units. Each elementary teacher unit was to receive $1,200 for the year beginning August 1, 1927, and $1,300, $1,400 and $1,500 for the years beginning August 1, 1928, 1929, and 1930, respectively. Each high school teacher unit was ordered to be given $1,600, $1,700, $1,800, and $1,900 for the years beginning August 1, 1927, 1928, 1929, and 1930, respectively. Both types of units were to receive the amounts allotted in 1930 during the years following. The required contribution of the local district was reduced from 1.5 mills on the actual valuation of taxable property to 0.6 mills.

Certain laws were passed in 1928 requiring publicity for annual estimates and budgets in fiscally independent cities and for accounts of monies expended, including all receipts and expenditures in all districts. In the case of publicity for annual estimates, the cities were required to publish statements in their official newspapers. Publicity for accounts of monies expended was ordered to be furnished by an annual financial report, by a special pamphlet, or by publication in an official paper. All districts were also obligated by law to give publicity to the details and purposes of bond issues.[64]

The equalization quotas were amended in 1929 to include all school districts employing two or more teachers for the legal school term, which provided for the academic instruction of pupils completing the work of the elementary grades. The amounts to be granted for each elementary and high school teacher unit were kept the same, but the high school units were amended to include part-time and continuation units. It was also decided that there should be deducted from these equalization quotas on the basis of teacher units an amount equal to the total of all sums paid out of public monies to the school district for the year for which the apportionment of the equalization quota was

[63] L. of N. Y., 1917, Chap. 794; 1927, Chap. 491, Sec. 1.
[64] L. of N. Y., 1928, Chap. 594, Sec. 1, and Chap. 595, Sec. 1.

approved *except* quotas concerning non-resident academic pupils, teacher-training classes, transportation, school buildings, and compensation for and expenses of attending teachers' conferences or institutes, plus an amount equal to 60 cents on each $1,000 of actual valuation of real and personal property. The balance, if any, was to be paid to the city or school district. The amount apportioned was not to be greater than the amount of excess of total expenditures for school purposes above the aggregate of the amount raised from a five-mill tax on actual valuation of taxable property and the public monies apportioned by law.[65] The sum of $1,000,000 was appropriated to carry out this act.[66]

School districts employing only one teacher were given special attention in 1929 when they were apportioned $1,300, $1,400 and $1,500 for the school years ending July 31, 1929, 1930, and 1931, respectively, minus the value of a four-mill tax on each dollar of actual valuation of taxable property. It was further provided that $1,500 minus the value of the four-mill tax should be granted for the years following 1931; that no one-teacher district should receive less than $425; that the amount allotted should not be greater than the excess of total expenditures for school purposes above the amount which would result from a tax of four mills on each dollar of actual valuation of taxable property; and that monies apportioned under the provisions of this section should be in lieu of all other apportionments except the transportation quota and the compensation for and expenses of attending teachers' conferences or institutes. The following section appropriated the sum of $2,050,000 to carry out the provisions of the act.[67]

State support for the instruction of children retarded in mental development was appropriated in 1929 by providing that the state would be responsible for one-half the salary up to $1,000 per teacher for teachers in charge of special classes for mentally retarded children.[68] Vocational schools and departments enrolling non-resident pupils received state aid under a law passed in 1929 giving them $50 per year for each non-resident academic pupil attending. This was merely extending the state tuition for non-resident academic pupils to include vocational schools and departments, as well as the high schools and academic departments previously mentioned.

[65] *L. of N. Y.*, 1929, Chap. 358, Sec. 1.   [66] *Ibid.*, Chap. 358, Sec. 2.
[67] *Ibid.*, Chap. 357, Sec. 1 and 2.   [68] *Ibid.*, Chap. 258, Sec. 2.

The legislation of 1930 was of special importance because of the number of quotas that were repealed in that year. The academic, district, supervision, teachers', and additional teachers' quotas were eliminated, except as they applied to central rural schools and consolidated districts. The following special quotas were also removed from the list of state apportionments: industrial education, mentally retarded, Americanization, school nurses, health teachers and health experts, and physically handicapped.

The transportation quota was extended in 1930 to include transportation outside the confines of a district:

Each district which does not maintain a high school shall provide transportation when necessary for its pupils who have completed the work of the eighth grade and are receiving academic instruction in another district. There shall be apportioned and paid to each such district a quota to be known as a transportation quota equivalent to one-half of the sum paid for such transportation, subject, however, to the approval of the commissioner of education.[69]

A new quota was enacted in 1930 for districts maintaining a home school and contracting with another district for the education of children who had not completed the eighth grade. It provided that the districts maintaining the home school should receive $25 per pupil when they contracted for fewer than ten pupils and that when the number was ten or more they should receive a quota on the basis of average daily attendance of all pupils in such district. The only financial aid formerly granted was $100, provided the home district contracted for twelve or more pupils. The paragraph relating to the total amount of state funds that a school district operating under the contract plan could receive was altered by shifting the basic tax from one-half of one per cent on the assessed valuation of the district to four mills on each dollar of actual valuation of taxable property. The agreement that a district contracting for the education of all its children of school age should receive the apportionments it would be entitled to if it maintained a school was continued, with the single amendment that the children must be given 190 days of schooling including legal holidays instead of 180 days as hitherto required.[70]

While the distribution of funds to the schools by the state had been based for many years on a year beginning July 1 and ending June 30, no law or laws had been written into the Education Law

[69] L. of N. Y., 1930, Chap. 263, Sec. 1.   [70] Ibid., Chap. 600, Sec. 1.

concerning the time of beginning and ending the school year until 1931. The legislature then decreed that:

> The term "school year" means the period commencing on the first day of July in each year and ending on the thirtieth day of June next following.[71]

The following law was passed by the 1933 legislature concerning when and how monies should be apportioned:

> At least one-half of the moneys so annually apportioned by the commissioner of education to cities and school districts not having a fiscal year identical with the calendar year shall be payable on or before the fifteenth day of January and the remaining part of such moneys on or before the fifteenth day of March, in each year, next after such apportionment, to the treasurer of the several counties and the said treasurer shall apply for and receive the same as soon as payable. The county treasurer shall pay to the city treasurer of each city and the treasurer of each union free school district and of each central school district, situated within his county, all school moneys apportioned to such city or district as provided by this chapter.
>
> At least six-tenths of the moneys so annually apportioned by the commissioner of education to cities having a fiscal year identical with the calendar year shall be payable on or before the first day of February, in each year, next after such apportionment, and four-tenths of such moneys on or before the first day of October to the city treasurer or chamberlain of each such city.[72]

This law penalized cities having fiscal years identical with the calendar year by delaying the delivery of their shares of the school monies. Delaying the payment of four-tenths of the money to which these school districts were entitled until October 1 benefited the state, as the state's fiscal year ends June 30 and this arrangement enabled the state to defer approximately $25,000,000 to the budget of the following fiscal year (1934).

The quota established in 1919 providing for the payment of ten cents a mile for traveling expenses and one dollar a day for each day or part of a day teachers spent in attending a conference or institute for which they were required to leave their own schools, was repealed in 1933 with a resultant saving to the state of approximately $100,000.[73] Items of support of the common schools, the academic quotas, appropriations for books, apparatus, standard works of art, and continuation schools were decreased 10 per cent from the amounts allowed under the 1932 state allotments. Transportation quotas, building quotas, and Indian

---

[71] L. of N. Y., 1931, Chap. 468, Sec. 1.   [72] L. of N. Y., 1933, Chap. 215, Sec. 1.
[73] Ibid., 1933, Chap. 224, Sec. 1. Soper, Wayne W., The Development of State Support of Education in New York State, p. 57.

school quotas were not lessened.[74] The quota concerning conference expenses was eliminated as explained heretofore. The training class quota first established in 1890 to help support one year of training beyond high school for prospective rural teachers was eliminated in 1933 by the Board of Regents.[75]

Central rural districts were entitled to receive the following apportionments under the 1933 law: grants to union free school districts, district quotas, teachers' quotas, additional teachers' quotas, equalization quotas, financial aid to consolidated districts, the transportation quota of one-half the amount spent, and the building quota of one-fourth the sum spent but not including as part of the sum spent any federal aid received.[76] Certain land areas were set aside in 1786 for the support of "gospel and schools." The 1932 legislature made provision that any "gospel funds" belonging to a school district which had become part of a central rural district should be paid to the treasurer of the central school district and used for school purposes.[77]

The limitations which had first been placed on the issuing of bonds by certain school districts in 1920 were altered in 1933 and the restrictions were made to apply to a larger number of districts. All districts having an assessed valuation of $100,000 or more were included under the new act. Bonds could not be sold to pay more than 6 per cent interest. The limit on total bonded indebtedness was continued at 15 per cent of the assessed valuation of real property within the districts, with the proviso, as before, that bonds in excess of that amount could be issued only by securing a two-thirds vote of qualified electors present at the meeting, in favor of a resolution authorizing such a bond issue. It was again declared that the last payment retiring a bond issue must come not more than thirty years from the date of authorization of the issue, and a new clause was introduced to the effect that the largest annual payment of principal and interest must not be more than 25 per cent in excess of the smallest prior annual installment.[78]

This description of the measures of financial support for public education developed during the period from 1900 to 1933 reveals the following tendencies: The establishment of minimum requirements which must be followed by the individual school districts

[74] L. of N. Y., 1933, Chap. 192, Sec. 1. [75] Soper, Wayne W., op. cit., p. 57.
[76] L. of N. Y., 1933, Chap. 823, Sec. 1. [77] L. of N. Y., 1786, Chap. 67; 1932, Chap. 186, Sec. 1.
[78] L. of N. Y., 1933, Chap. 339, Sec. 1.

in order to qualify for the apportionment concerned; the encouragement by subsidies for local districts to merge and form larger districts; the modification of methods of apportionment of school monies more nearly to provide equality of educational opportunity and support; the development of control of some aspects of public school finance; and the provision of an increasing amount of money for the operation of the public school system.

Evaluation in Terms of the Criteria

The motivating influence behind every one of these tendencies was that of providing, as far as possible, for equality of educational opportunity and support. The minimum requirements which were set up in regard to size of class, length of term, salary paid, course of study followed, and the like, were to a large degree concerned with giving each child as good schooling as that provided elsewhere in the state. The many quotas granted "central rural districts," "central high school districts," and "consolidated districts," encouraging the abolition of small districts through consolidation, were created for the purpose of securing more equitable support and educational opportunity. The continuous change in the methods of apportioning state funds, especially since 1925, has sought to achieve a minimum program and an equitable basis for distribution of state funds for school purposes.

The control, which has been centralized in the Commissioner of Education as head of the State Education Department, over publicity for the accounting for school monies, bond issues, city salary schedules, and the teachers' retirement system, seeks in each instance to provide equality of educational opportunity but does not have any direct relationship to the problem of support except in the case of the state teachers' retirement system where the state's contribution to each individual account is based on the salary earned and is considered to be an equitable means of calculating the share of the state. The increase in the amount of state apportionments to local districts has some bearing on the problems of equality of opportunity and support, especially as considered under the tendency already discussed for the state to modify or change its basis of apportionment.

All the tendencies described may be classed as pertaining to the *externa* of education in so far as they deal with the financing of public education. Some of the quotas which were awarded only if the local district complied with certain minimum requirements contained curriculum prescriptions. These mandatory influences on the courses of study offered are weighed with reference to the criteria stated in the section of this chapter entitled "Curriculum."

Local initiative and opportunity for experimentation were not taken away by any of the tendencies except the fourth, dealing with the state's control of certain financial matters. A local district might wish to issue bonds for more than 15 per cent of their assessed valuation without first obtaining a two-thirds vote of the qualified voters present at the meeting, but the loss of freedom involved seems small compared with the reasonableness of the requirement. Cities desiring salary schedules other than those adopted by the state legislature may obtain them by means of special legislation, or by such extra-legal devices as requiring contributions of certain percentages of the salaries paid, as many cities now are doing. Districts, overcome by the illusion of economy resulting from the founding of a local teachers' retirement association rather than utilizing the facilities of the State Teachers' Retirement System, are fortunate to be in a position where local initiative and opportunity for experimentation are denied.

None of these tendencies operate to favor one aspect or type of education at the expense of the rest of the program.

THE UNIVERSITY OF THE STATE OF NEW YORK

The "Unification Act" of 1904, which set up a single administrative authority in place of the two previously existing, created the position of Commissioner of Education and defined his powers in the following words:

> The office of superintendent of public instruction and the office of secretary of the Board of Regents shall be abolished from and after April one, nineteen hundred and four, and the powers and duties of said offices shall be exercised and performed by the commissioner of education. All the powers and duties of the Board of Regents in relation to the supervision of elementary and secondary schools including all schools, except colleges, technical and professional schools, are hereby devolved upon the commissioner of education.

The Commissioner of Education was made the executive officer of the Board of Regents and was empowered to create departments, appoint deputies, choose heads of departments, and fix salaries.[79]

[79] *L. of N. Y.*, 1904, Chap. 40, Sec. 4.

Two new divisions were added to the State Education Department in 1911 to take over activities which had formerly been performed outside the department. The state historian was made the chief of the newly organized division of history and the supervisor of public records became the first chief of the division of public records.[80]

The establishment of the "State Teachers' Retirement Fund" for public school teachers in 1911 enlarged the duties of the State Education Department to include receiving the contributions made by teachers; investing the monies in the fund; receiving donations, legacies, gifts, and bequests; receiving appropriations made by the state legislature for the fund; managing the fund; and paying monies to individuals entitled to refunds or retirement allowances.[81]

The office of "District Superintendent of Schools" came into being on January 1, 1912, through the carrying out of a law setting up the position in 1910. Qualifications for the position were that the applicant be twenty-one years old, a citizen of the United States, a resident of the state, possess a certificate authorizing the holder to teach in the state, and pass an examination on the supervision of courses of study in agriculture and the teaching of agriculture.[82]

State scholarships for honorably discharged soldiers, sailors, and marines were provided in 1919 for veterans who could meet the qualifications prescribed by the Commissioner of Education, who was vested with the responsibility of drawing up rules and regulations and holding competitive examinations at least once a year. The Commissioner was also given the power to revoke for cause any scholarship awarded.[83] The law was amended in 1920 to include trained nurses under its provisions. At the same time a limit of three years was set on the length of time that any one individual might receive one of the scholarship awards.[84] In 1930 a phrase was added further changing the law of 1919 concerning the scholarships so that the following groups were eligible to apply for scholarships:

. . . and [for] children of such soldiers, sailors, and marines who died while serving in the armed forces of the United States or as a result thereof.

[80] L. of N. Y., 1911, Chap. 380, Sec. 3. [81] Ibid., Chap. 449, Sec. 1.
[82] L. of N. Y., 1910, Vol. 2, Chap. 607, Sec. 1. [83] L. of N. Y., 1919, Vol. 2, Chap. 606, Sec. 1.
[84] L. of N. Y., 1920, Vol. 3, Chap. 893, Sec. 1.

The New York State School for the Blind at Batavia was transferred to the University of the State of New York from the State Board of Charities and all powers of regulation, supervision, and control were vested in the Commissioner of Education. However, the State Board of Charities was still allowed to visit and to inspect the school, and the fiscal control was left in the hands of the Fiscal Supervisor of State Charities.[85]

The Advisory Commission for the Rehabilitation of Physically Handicapped Persons was created in 1920 with the following membership: the Commissioner of Education, chairman; one member of the State Industrial Commission designated to serve by the Governor; the Commissioner of Health; and the secretary, an officer of the State Education Department designated by the Commissioner of Education. The Advisory Commission made it optional with the person concerned whether or not he took the special training offered. The State Education Department was asked to assume the following duties: Provide special courses in the public schools; pay private schools or private employers for courses when they are acceptable and when it seems better to make use of them than to begin such a course in the public schools; maintain social service to visit homes during and after the special training; aid in securing employment; purchase needed crutches, wooden legs, braces, and such, at cost; make surveys and studies and coöperate with any department or agency of the state which can furnish information or help. The sum of $75,000 was appropriated, and the Board of Regents in its capacity as the State Board for Vocational Education agreed to accept the provisions of any Federal law appropriating funds for rehabilitation work.[86]

The financial powers of the University of the State of New York were increased by the 1920 legislature as follows:

> The said corporation shall have power to take, hold and administer real and personal property and the income thereof in trust for any educational, scientific, historical, or other purpose within the jurisdiction of the Regents of the University of the State of New York.[87]

One of the greatest increases in the scope of the authority of the University of the State of New York came in 1921 when all schools and classes in the state regardless of type were placed under its licensing power:

[85] L. of N. Y., 1919, Vol. 1, Chap. 136, Sec. 1.   [86] L. of N. Y., 1920, Vol. 3, Chap. 700, Sec. 1.
[87] Ibid., Vol. 1, Chap. 161, Sec. 1.

No person, firm, corporation, association, or society shall conduct, maintain, or operate any school, institute, class, or course of instruction in any subjects whatever without making application for and being granted a license from the University of the State of New York to so conduct, maintain, or operate such institute, school, class, or course.

Exceptions were made covering private schools or educational institutions already members of the University, classes operated by fraternal orders for instructing candidates in rituals, and schools established by recognized religious denominations. The licensing rules were left to the discretion of the Regents. Schools or classes applying for licenses had to submit a verified statement of purpose, and it was legislated that no license would be issued to any school or class teaching the overthrow of organized government by force or to any school, institute, class, or course conducted in a fraudulent manner. The right to revoke licenses was reserved, and conducting a school without a license was made a misdemeanor punishable by a $100 fine or by a sixty-day jail sentence. Ten thousand dollars was appropriated to carry the provisions of the act into effect.[88]

In 1923 the University was given one more educational activity over which to watch when the New York State Nautical School, organized in 1913, was placed under the general supervision of the Commissioner of Education. The board of governors of the school was continued, but the Commissioner of Education was granted the right to direct that the actions and expenditures of the board of governors meet with his approval.[89]

While the 1921 act relating to the licensing power of the University of the State of New York seemed to be all-inclusive, a new section was added in 1923 dealing specifically with correspondence schools:

No person, firm, or corporation shall conduct in this state a correspondence school unless such person, firm, or corporation shall first have secured the approval of the Board of Regents. Such approval shall be secured and granted in accordance with rules and regulations to be adopted by such board. Violation of this section shall constitute a misdemeanor.[90]

The supervision and licensing powers of the University were extended in 1927 to include chiropody, dental societies and the practice of dentistry, optometry, pharmacy, practice of medicine

---

[88] *L. of N. Y.*, 1921, Vol. 3, Chap. 667, Sec. 1, 2, and 3 (79).
[89] *L. of N. Y.*, 1923, Chap. 398, Sec. 1.   [90] *Ibid.*, Chap. 593, Sec. 1.

and veterinary medicine and surgery, formerly part of the public health laws; and certified shorthand reporters, engineers and surveyors, public accountants, and registered architects formerly regulated under the general business law. The articles of the public health law and the general business law dealing with these occupations were repealed, and it was ruled that none of the boards concerned should gain any new authority because of the transfer of these provisions to the education law.[91]

The financial incentives which were offered to encourage consolidation of school districts have been discussed earlier in this chapter. The regulation by the University of the number of supervisory districts, with the suggestion that the number might be diminished, is found in an act of the 1933 legislature:

Whenever a vacancy hereafter occurs in the office of district superintendent of schools in any supervisory district, the department of education shall survey the field in the country where the vacancy occurred, and if it shall find that the continuance of the number of supervisory districts then existing is no longer necessary to serve adequately the educational interests of the county it shall by order, notwithstanding any other provision of this chapter to the contrary, redistrict the county so as to provide for a lesser number of supervisory districts. Such order shall be filed in the office of the clerk of the county.

Prior to April 1, 1936, the department of education shall survey the field in each county of the state, and if it shall find that the educational interests of any county will be adequately served by a lesser number of supervisory districts than the number to which it is entitled on January 1, 1936, such department shall by order, notwithstanding any other provisions of this chapter to the contrary, redistrict such county so as to provide for a lesser number of supervisory districts. Such order shall be filed in the office of the clerk of the county on or before April 1, 1936.[92]

Since the "Unification Act" of 1904, setting up a single board with one executive officer in place of the two administrative agencies formerly in charge of public education, the University of the State of New York has grown in power, in size of staff, and in the appropriations for its support until it is now one of the most important divisions of the government of New York State. The various appropriations for the support of the public school system are taken up in this act under the heading of "financial support," the matters concerning the supervision of teacher training under "teacher training and certification," and the relationship of the University to the public school curriculum may be

[91] *L. of N. Y.*, 1927, Chap. 153, Sec. 1, 2, 3, and 4.   [92] *L. of N. Y.*, 1933, Chap. 218, Sec. 1.

found under the title, "curriculum and types of schools." Each of these three topics is concerned with tendencies in administration which might be included under the consideration of the University of the State of New York. For the sake of convenience in applying the criteria, tendencies are divided among these three topics. This organization of materials is mentioned here so that there will be no possibility of conveying the impression that the items described under "The University of the State of New York" are the only ones over which the University has jurisdiction.

Evaluation in Terms of the Criteria

Equality of educational opportunity and support, the first criterion, can be applied to only certain of the legal changes discussed. The creation of the office of district superintendent of schools, the placing of the State School for the Blind under the University, the provision for special public school courses for physically handicapped children, the requirement that all schools including correspondence schools must be licensed by the University, and the power granted the State Education Department to redistrict counties were all administrative changes directed toward the ideal of equality of educational opportunity. None of these tendencies discussed under this section had much to do with the support of public education. The provision of scholarships for soldiers, sailors, marines, trained nurses, and the children of soldiers, sailors, and marines favored certain groups and was in contradiction to the ideal of equality of opportunity.

Local initiative and opportunity for experimentation were not affected by any of the acts reported in this section of the chapter except the one creating a State Teachers' Retirement Fund. The relationship of local initiative to this centralizing tendency has already been set forth under the first section of this chapter, "State Support."

All the matters discussed in this section seem chiefly to be concerned with the *externa* of education. The jurisdiction of the University of the State of New York over the School for the Blind at Batavia does not appear to include control of the curriculum, and the State Education Department's connection with courses for physically handicapped persons through its two members on the Advisory Commission for the Rehabilitation of Physically

Handicapped Persons does not necessarily imply that the content of the special courses approved will be dictated by the State Education Department.

None of the administrative changes described favored one aspect or phase of the educational program at the expense of the whole program. The arrangements for caring for the blind and the physically handicapped were made for the purpose of providing those individuals with a more nearly equal opportunity, compared with normal individuals, of acquiring a public school education.

REGENTS EXAMINATIONS

The system of Regents Examinations was first established in 1865 for the purpose of maintaining standards in the academies of the state and securing a uniform basis on which to make apportionments of school monies. The original examinations dealt with arithmetic, English grammar, geography, and spelling. In 1877 the examinations were extended to include the so-called academic studies.[93] Whereas in 1878 the examinations were offered in only twenty subjects, by 1896 the number had been increased to eighty.

Regents diplomas were first issued in 1880 to those passing the number of subjects considered as standard for graduation from a high school. The Regents examination system was extended in 1882 to include those desiring to study for admission to the New York Bar if they were not college graduates. In 1889 candidates for the medical degree were required to submit either a Regents certificate or a college diploma.[94]

In 1894 the dental schools in the state adopted the Regents' credentials as a requirement for admission, and in 1895 a legislative enactment stipulated the same educational standard for dental and veterinarian students as had been required for medical students.[95]

A system of examinations for individuals desiring to become public accountants was adopted by legislative mandate in 1896.

The Regents Examinations during the present century have had a profound influence upon the courses of study offered by public school districts throughout the state. The use of Regents' credits for determining the issuance of a high school diploma for

[93] *L. of N. Y.*, 1877, Chap. 425.   [94] *L. of N. Y.*, 1889, Chap. 468.
[95] *L. of N. Y.*, 1895, Chap. 626 and 860.

college entrance purposes and as a measure of evaluating the work of school teachers and systems, has tended to limit the curricular material offered to that which will most adequately prepare for the examinations given by the Regents. Although local school districts are permitted to do the preliminary grading of examinations, the final grades are determined by the Examinations Division of the University of the State of New York. This state grading tends to be inflexible. An illustration of the inflexibility of state grading may be found in a case where no credit was given for problems solved by a method other than the one favored by the state authorities, even though the correct answers to the problems were obtained.

Evaluation in Terms of the Criteria

It is evident that the Regents Examinations have had at least as great an effect upon the subject matter taught in the localities of the state as any of the mandatory curriculum provisions which have been enacted. The Regents Examinations help to bring about equality of educational opportunity in those communities which would not otherwise provide reasonably good courses of study. They are concerned with the *interna* of education, although the more progressive school systems seldom have to alter their educational offerings because of them. The effect of these examinations upon local school systems tends to be greatest when the local administrative unit is too small or too poverty stricken, or both, to employ adequate professional leadership.

JUDICIAL POWER OF THE COMMISSIONER OF EDUCATION

The judicial power of the Commissioner of Education of New York State has been of vital importance in interpreting and enforcing legislation relating to the public schools. The State Superintendent was given the power of appellate jurisdiction in 1822 and the chief state school officer has continued to hold this power to the present time, with the exception of the years 1849–1853. The Commissioner was granted the power of original jurisdiction by legislative enactment of 1910.[96] When the courts have once assumed jurisdiction, the Commissioner will not consider a case, but the courts sometimes review decisions given by the Commissioner in spite of the fact that his decisions are supposed to be

[96] *L. of N. Y.*, 1910, Chap. 140.

"final." Brubacher makes the following statement in his study of the judicial power of the Commissioner of Education of New York State:

> In spite of the clear and strong language used in the statute, the legislative fiat that the commissioner's decisions are beyond review really barks more menacingly than a procession of court decisions in the twentieth century have let it bite. These cases have come to the court of appeals in various ways, sometimes by *certiorari*, to review the commissioner's decisions; sometimes by a writ of prohibition, to prevent the commissioner from enforcing his decision; and other times a review becomes necessary when the superintendent's decision is presented as a bar to the relief sought by the plaintiff. Whether and to what degree the courts will allow this provision to have full literal operation has come to follow much the same reasoning employed in determining the question of concurrent and exclusive original jurisdiction. If the commissioner's decision concerns matters of internal administration of the school system of the state, and only incidentally, if at all, property rights, the general policy of the courts is not to review it. But the courts do not seem to think themselves excluded from reviewing even this type of case, at least where it appears that the commissioner has acted illegally, with "gross abuse of authority," or without jurisdiction.[97]

Decisions have been handed down by the Commissioner on such matters as alteration of school districts, consolidation of school districts, charge for non-resident tuition, provision for transportation, revocation of teachers' licenses, and the application of tenure laws. Legislative acts, court decisions, and precedents established by former decisions of the chief state school official aid the Commissioner in the utilization of his judicial powers. Sometimes, however, the decisions concern matters for which there are no precedents in educational law or prior decisions. Examples are given by Brubacher:

> . . . such appeals as those involving the right of teachers to wear distinctive religious garb, the compatibility of professional duties with those of maternity, and the requirement of school districts to provide by contract for opportunities of instruction on the secondary or academic grade.[98]

Evaluation in Terms of the Criteria

The judicial power of the Commissioner of Education has aided in the effort to secure equality of educational opportunity and support when it has enabled the Commissioner to render decisions concerning the necessity for maintaining public schools, the

[97] Brubacher, John S., *The Judicial Power of the New York State Commissioner of Education*, pp. 59–60.   [98] *Ibid.*, p. 165.

legality of state minimum requirements, and the plans and specifications for school buildings. Sometimes it has worked against equalization of opportunity in making possible such decisions as those made prior to 1913 relating to consolidation of districts.[99] This judicial power has usually been related to the whole program of public education and has not often taken away opportunity for local initiative, as cases may be appealed either to the courts or to the Commissioner and may sometimes be brought into the courts after the Commissioner's decision has been given. The judicial power of the Commissioner has usually been applied to *externa*.

TEACHER TRAINING

In the introduction to this chapter there are discussed the various apportionments which were awarded to further the cause of teacher training prior to 1900. In 1900, $320,000 was appropriated for the support of the state normal and training schools. The allocation of this sum was in charge of the State Superintendent of Public Instruction. Teachers' institutes and the so-called "summer institutes" which had their beginnings in 1894 and 1896, respectively, received for their support the sum of $50,000.[100] The twelve state normal schools, the Indian schools, and the institutions for the instruction of the deaf, dumb, and blind shared $320,000 in 1901.[101] Fifty thousand dollars was also appropriated for the professional training of teachers and for the maintenance of teacher-training classes in academies and union free schools.[102] A new method of awarding funds for the support of teacher training was established in 1909 by the following act:

The commissioner of education shall apportion the money annually appropriated for the support of training of teachers as follows:

1. To each academy and union free school district which has maintained a training class in accordance with the provisions of article twenty-five of this chapter and with the regulations prescribed by the commissioner of education, the sum of seven hundred dollars.
2. The balance of the money appropriated for such purpose shall be apportioned to the cities of the state which maintain training schools in accordance

[99] Brubacher, John S., *op. cit.*, p. 57.
[100] *L. of N. Y.*, 1900, Vol. 2, Chap. 418; 1894, Chap. 556; 1896, Chap. 156.
[101] *L. of N. Y.*, 1901, Vol. 2, Chap. 644, Sec. 1.   [102] *Ibid.*, Chap. 645, Sec. 1.

with the provisions of articles twenty-one and twenty-five of this chapter and with the regulations prescribed by the commissioner of education, ratable according to the aggregate attendance of the pupils regularly admitted to such training schools.[103]

The minimum size of class was set at ten and the minimum term was ruled to be thirty-six weeks, but provision was included whereby the Commissioner of Education might permit a term shorter than the prescribed minimum or an enrollment less than the minimum required and allow a proportionate sum of money. The Commissioner of Education was also given the power to set up rules and regulations, the details concerning admission to training classes, and the course of instruction to be followed.

Additional teacher-training facilities were provided in 1918 to prepare teachers for giving instruction to the illiterate.

The commissioner of education is also authorized and empowered to organize, maintain, and operate training institutes and regular courses of study in connection with the state normal institutions and in the cities of the state for the purpose of training regular public school teachers and others in the best methods to be pursued in giving instruction to illiterates over sixteen years of age.[104]

Twenty thousand dollars was appropriated to be expended by the Commissioner of Education in this way.

The compulsory course in physical training for all pupils above eight years of age attending public schools, which was introduced in 1918, required specially qualified teachers to make it worth while. The state granted financial aid to districts employing teachers licensed under the regulations of the Regents to teach physical education, and also appropriated $60,000 for the supervision and training of teachers of physical education. The supervision and special instruction were to be supplied by the State Education Department.[105]

The "institute quota," previously discussed under the section on "State Support," aided teachers by providing for the payment of 10 cents a mile traveling expenses and one dollar a day extra compensation to teachers attending an institute or conference at any place other than the location of their schools, when they were required to attend by law or by regulation of the State Education Department.[106]

An act of 1920 established twenty-five industrial teachers'

---

[103] *L. of N. Y.*, 1909, Chap. 406, Sec. 1.
[105] *Ibid.*, Chap. 442, Sec. 1 and 2.
[104] *L. of N. Y.*, 1918, Vol. 2, Chap. 412, Sec. 1.
[106] *L. of N. Y.*, 1919, Vol. 1, Chap. 109, Sec. 1.

scholarships worth not more than $2,000 each for the maintenance and support of those chosen at the vocational department of any New York state normal school or schools for one year. Candidates for these scholarships had to offer as one of their qualifications five years of successful experience in trade, industry, or technical occupation.[107] These scholarships were considered under the sections on "State Support" and are again brought up in this section because of the fact that they were granted to teachers of a special type of education.

The teacher-training-class quota, established in 1890 for the support of training classes in academies and union free school districts, was increased from $700 to $1,200 by the 1923 legislature.[108] The 1925 legislature increased this quota to $2,000 with the proviso that teachers of training classes should receive at least $1,800 a year, and that the quota would only be granted to one hundred such classes.[109] The quota was finally repealed in 1933 long after the state normal schools and teachers colleges had taken over the training of the large majority of candidates for teaching positions.[110]

Evaluation in Terms of the Criteria

All of these centralizing tendencies having to do with teacher training have aided in bringing about equality of educational opportunity by the provisions which they made for seeing to it that enough trained individuals were available to fill the teaching positions of the state.

The majority of these state influences on teacher training were concerned with the whole program rather than with any particular phase of it. The training institutes and courses of study which the Commissioner of Education was authorized to organize were necessary for training teachers in the best methods of instructing illiterates. The supervision and instruction which were provided for the teachers of physical training were no more than necessary properly to qualify them for teaching the subject. The industrial teachers scholarships were provided to meet the need for more teachers for vocational schools, and probably were necessary to secure the type and length of experience which was wanted, namely, five years of successful experience in trade, industrial, or technical occupations.

107 L. of N. Y., 1920, Vol. 3, Chap. 853, Sec. 1.   108 L. of N. Y., 1923, Chap. 162, Sec. 1.
109 L. of N. Y., 1925, Chap. 152, Sec. 1.   110 L. of N. Y., 1933, Chap. 218.

None of these activities of the state concerned with the training of teachers set up other than minimum standards. Local initiative and opportunity for experimentation were preserved for each or any locality to go beyond the standards established by the state with regard to the qualifications and training of teachers. The centralizing tendencies which have occurred in teacher training have been a good influence on the public school system of New York State.

THE CURRICULUM

At the beginning of the century New York State had regulations forbidding the teaching of sectarian doctrine and requiring instruction in arithmetic, English, geography, penmanship, reading, spelling, and physiology and hygiene. No important changes were made in regard to required subjects or types of schools until 1915, when the farm schools were established. These schools were to give instruction in the trades and industrial, agricultural, and homemaking subjects to children from eight to eighteen years of age. Their organization was encouraged by the state aid granted to them if they maintained an enrollment of fifteen pupils and a term of not less than thirty-six weeks. Although considered by law as a part of the public school system, it was provided that the parents were to pay the expenses of the pupils in these schools whenever they could do so.[111]

The 1916 legislature introduced a compulsory course in physical training and gave the Board of Regents the duty of adopting rules to determine the subjects to be included, the qualifications of teachers, and the attendance regulations. It was stipulated that the instruction in physical training should average twenty minutes a day. State aid was created for all approved teachers employed in teaching courses in physical training.[112] A Military Training Commission was established, and one of its duties was to confer with the Board of Regents concerning courses in physical training. After September 1, 1916, all boys over sixteen and not more than nineteen years of age, except those employed or those exempt by the military training commission, were required to take part in military training activities for a minimum of three hours each week during the school or college year.[113]

The Commissioner of Education and the Regents of the Univer-

---

[111] L. of N. Y., 1915, Vol. 2, Chap. 307, Sec. 1.   [112] L. of N. Y., 1916, Vol. 3, Chap. 567, Sec. 1.
[113] Ibid., Chap. 566, Sec. 1.

sity of the State of New York were empowered in 1917 to prescribe regulations for ascertaining the number of children in each school district in the state who were three or more years retarded in mental development. The school districts were to be given until May 18, 1918, to make lists of all children three or more years mentally retarded. Boards of education finding ten or more such children were ordered to establish special classes for their education with not more than fifteen children in any one class. Provision was made whereby boards of education having fewer than ten mentally retarded children might contract with some other board of education for their instruction.[114]

The provisions of the national Act concerning vocational education, which was passed and approved February 23, 1917, were accepted by New York State the same year. The State Treasurer was appointed custodian of all monies which might be paid the state for vocational education, and the Board of Regents were designated the State Board for Vocational Education with full authorization to coöperate with the Federal Board for Vocational Education in the administration of the provisions of the act.[115] The military training commission recognized the importance of federally aided vocational education by the following enactment:

Such requirement as to military training, herein prescribed, may in the discretion of the commission be met in part by such vocational training or vocational experience as will, in the opinion of the commission, specifically prepare boys of the ages named for service useful to the state, in the maintenance of defence, in the promotion of public safety, in the conservation and development of the state's resources, or in the construction and maintenance of public improvements.[116]

Boards of education of each city and each union free school district and trustees of each common school district were required, by act of the 1917 legislature, to ascertain by May 18, 1918, the number of children under eighteen years of age, deaf, blind, crippled, or otherwise so physically defective as to be unable to enroll in regular classes in the public school system. School districts finding ten or more children were required to establish special classes to provide instruction suitable to the mental and physical abilities of the children. School areas with fewer than ten physically defective children were permitted to contract with some other board of education for their instruction.[117]

[114] L. of N. Y., 1917, Vol. 2, Chap. 553, Sec. 1.   [115] Ibid., Vol. 2, Chap. 576, Sec. 1.
[116] Ibid., Vol. 1, Chap. 49, Sec. 1.   [117] Ibid., Vol. 2, Chap. 559, Sec. 1.

Instruction in the humane treatment of animals and birds was made a part of the state prescribed courses of study by the following article added to the Education Law in 1917:

The officer, board, or commission authorized or required to prescribe courses of instruction shall cause instruction to be given in every elementary school under state control or supported wholly or partly by public money of the state, in the humane treatment and protection of animals and birds and the importance of the part they play in the economy of nature. Such instruction shall be for such period of time during each school year as the board of regents may prescribe and may be joined with work in literature, reading, language, nature study, or ethnology. Such weekly instruction may be divided into two or more periods. A school district shall not be entitled to participate in the public school money on account of any school or the attendance at any school subject to the provisions of this section, if the instruction hereby required is not given therein. The commissioner of education shall, pursuant to this act, cause the consideration of the humane treatment of animals and birds to be included in the program of teachers' institutes.[118]

Beginning September 1, 1918, all pupils over eight years of age in both public and private schools were required to attend classes in instruction in patriotism and citizenship as part of their school programs. The Board of Regents were allotted the duty of determining the subjects to be included in the courses of study for each grade and the period of time to be utilized. The Commissioner of Education was held responsible for enforcing the law and was granted the right to withhold public school money in case school authorities failed to provide for such instruction and to compel the children to attend. The Commissioner of Education was also directed to take charge of the inspection and supervision of this instruction in patriotism and citizenship.[119]

The military training commission was abolished in 1921, but courses in physical training for boys and girls over eight years of age were continued. The Regents were still charged with the task of determining the subjects to be included in the teaching of physical training courses, the qualifications of the teachers, the period of instruction, and the like.[120]

Courses for the instruction of foreign born and native adults and minors over sixteen years of age were provided for by legislation passed in 1921. The following excerpt from the law gives the main provisions:

[118] *L. of N. Y.*, 1917, Vol. 1, Chap. 210, Sec. 3.
[119] *L. of N. Y.*, 1918, Vol. 2, Chap. 241, Sec. 1 and 2.
[120] *L. of N. Y.*, 1921, Vol. 1, Chap. 211, Sec. 1.

The commissioner of education or the board of education or trustees of any city or school district may provide for the establishment of courses of instruction or study in schools in connection with factories, places of employment, or in such other places as he or they may deem advisable, for the purpose of giving instruction to foreign born and native adults and minors over the age of sixteen years. Such course of instruction and study shall be prescribed by the Regents of the University of the State of New York, and shall be in conformity with rules to be adopted by them.[121]

The last sentence of the act provided state aid equal to one-half the salary paid to each teacher up to a maximum of $1,000 aid for any one teacher so employed.

Legislation permitting the establishment of home schools for the instruction of truants and delinquents in trade, industrial, agricultural, and homemaking subjects, as well as in the public school subjects, by a majority vote of the common council of any city of the second class was enacted in 1922. Such schools were to admit children of the city concerned and other children from eight to eighteen years of age. All home schools organized under this act were to be considered a part of the public school system and were ruled to be subject to the supervision and control of the Commissioner of Education and the State Education Department.[122]

A course of instruction in fire prevention was required by the legislature of 1923. The Commissioner of Education was to prescribe the course and it was to relate to the protection of life and property against loss or damage as a result of a preventable fire. The course was to be given in all public, private, and parochial schools for a period of not less than fifteen minutes each week of the school year.[123]

Instruction in the history and meaning of the provisions of the Constitution of the United States was prescribed in 1924. The law requiring this instruction was couched in the same terms as the 1918 act introducing instruction in patriotism and citizenship. All schools, including private schools, were to make the teaching of the history and meaning of the provisions of the United States Constitution part of the course of study for all pupils in the eighth grade and beyond. The Regents were to determine the subjects to be included and the period of instruction

[121] L. of N. Y., 1921, Vol. 2, Chap. 327, Sec. 1.
[122] L. of N. Y., 1922, Vol. 1, Chap. 465, Sec. 1 and 16.
[123] L. of N. Y., 1923, Chap. 397, Sec. 1.

in each grade. The Commissioner of Education was held responsible for the enforcement of the act and for the inspection and supervision of the instruction given. The power of withholding public money was granted to the Commissioner to force such instruction to be provided, to compel attendance, and so forth.[124] The public school system of the state was first required to provide instruction in the use and display of the flag in 1924 when the following law was enacted:

It shall be the duty of the commissioner of education to prepare, for the use of the public schools of the state, a program providing for a salute to the flag, for instruction in its correct use and display and such other patriotic exercises as may be deemed by him to be expedient, under such regulations and instructions as may best meet the varied requirements of the different grades in such school.[125]

The "physically defective" group of children previously referred to was divided into two groups by an enactment in 1925:

A "physically handicapped child" is one who, by reason of a physical defect or infirmity, whether congenital or acquired by accident, injury, or disease, is or may be expected to be totally or partially incapacitated for education or for remunerative occupation, but shall not include the deaf and blind.[126]

The act then went on to care for "physically handicapped" children as follows:

They shall have power to provide for physically handicapped children, transportation, home teaching, special classes or special schools, scholarships in nonresidence schools, tuition or tuition and maintenance in elementary, secondary, higher, special, and technical schools and, on recommendation of the state department of health, surgical, medical, or therapeutic treatment, hospital care, crutches, braces, and other appliances.[127]

The requirement that classes in physical training average twenty minutes a day for each school day, which was first introduced at the time of the passing of the original law in 1916, was omitted in the act concerning the teaching of physical education which was approved by the legislature of 1925.[128]

Provision was made in 1926 whereby the board of supervisors of any county might, by a majority vote, establish a county vocational education and extension board to give instruction in agriculture, home economics, and other special subjects approved by the Commissioner of Education. Such boards, if established,

124 *L. of N. Y.*, 1923, 1924, Chap. 64, Sec. 1.   125 *Ibid.*, Chap. 525, Sec. 1.
126 *Ibid.*, 1925, Chap. 227, Sec. 1.   127 *Ibid.*   128 *Ibid.*, Chap. 662, Sec. 1.

were required to have their courses approved by the Commissioner of Education and, when such courses were given in elementary or secondary schools, by the superintendent of schools concerned. The qualifications of all teachers employed were to conform to the regulations of the Board of Regents and the Commissioner of Education. These county vocational boards were to make annual reports to the Regents and to the board of supervisors of their county, and other reports as requested by the Commissioner of Education or by the board of supervisors.[129]

Evaluation in Terms of the Criteria

The chief centralizing tendencies affecting curriculum matters have been the addition of certain courses by request of the legislature, the establishing of courses and schools to care for children physically, mentally, or morally handicapped, and the acceptance of federal aid for vocation education on a "matching" basis.

The courses added, which deal with physical training, treatment of animals, patriotism and citizenship, fire prevention, Constitution of the United States, and the use of the flag, have not promoted equality of educational opportunity, opportunity for local initiative, or the development of the whole program of education. They have been concerned with the *interna* of education, with what is taught and, in those cases where time requirements are included, with the length of the periods of instruction.

The establishment of courses and schools for the many types of handicapped children has aided in securing equality of educational opportunity for the children attending. The rules and regulations set up by the Board of Regents have taken away much of the opportunity for local initiative. The special aid and attention devoted to this phase of the educational program have not been concerned with the needs of the whole program. These courses and school organizations have been *interna* in so far as they have had to do with what is to be taught and how it is to be "put across" to the children.

The acceptance of the offer of the Federal Board for Vocational Education, obligating the state to raise the same sum of money as that received from the board and permitting the employees of the board to supervise the spending of the total monies thus accumulated, did not further the ideals of educational equality and sup-

---

[129] *L. of N. Y.*, 1926, Chap. 505, Sec. 1.

port as similar arrangements were not made for other types of education. Local initiative was superseded not by state but by national authority. The "whole program" was sacrificed by this securing of money from the Federal Government which earmarked a like amount of state funds for a specific phase of education. Since the act provided for the approval by the Federal Board for Vocational Education of any courses of a vocational nature which might be established with the aid of the funds granted, it affected one of the *interna* of education in thus seeking to control subject matter and methods of instruction.

SUMMARY

New York State has been handicapped in its attempt to provide for equality of educational support by the large number and many types of local districts which have prevailed throughout the state.[130]   The recent repeal of many of the special quotas formerly provided has aided in the simplification of the system of state support. The large powers vested in the Commissioner of Education and in the University of the State of New York have aided in centralizing in the state educational officials authority over the state school system.

The curriculum prescriptions have been few in number, but the Regents Examinations have operated to establish state-determined courses of study in the majority of the school districts.

Minimum standards have been established in many matters of *externa* and have been inaugurated in several instances by special quotas granted for carrying them out.   The progress in abolishing small local units of administration has been slow and the present policy is to make consolidation profitable to participating districts.

[130] Chapter 328 of the *Laws of 1917* carried a provision for the establishment of town boards of education.   This provision was repealed by Chapter 199 of the *Laws of 1918*.

CHAPTER V

CONCLUSIONS

In 1897 Webster's study pointed out the decline of the "district system" and the increase in state control over textbooks, courses of study, certification of teachers, compulsory attendance, and length of the school term.[1] The district system is still very much in evidence in New York, while the county system which prevails in Maryland and North Carolina existed in these states when Webster's study was published. Maryland and New York still allow administrative units within the state to adopt textbooks of their choice. In Maryland the county is the unit of textbook uniformity and free books are mandatory, whereas in New York school districts select whatever books they desire and furnish them to the pupils free of charge only if they wish to do so. The desire of public school systems in New York State to achieve good records on the Regents Examinations somewhat narrows the field of textbooks from which selections are made. At present, North Carolina has state adoption of textbooks for elementary schools, whereas at the time of Webster's study county adoption was the order of the day.

The increase in state control of courses of study, which Webster included in his list of centralizing tendencies, has also been one of the important centralizing tendencies since 1900 in the states of Maryland, North Carolina, and New York. The increase in the number of prescribed subjects, except in Maryland, and the tendency to make the curriculum requirements more detailed and specific by such devices as the determination by the state of the length of time which a subject should be taught, are examples of methods used to control the content of the curriculum.

Certification of teachers in North Carolina and Maryland has been centralized in the State Department of Education since 1897 when Webster suggested that centralization was changing the relationship existing between certification and the state authori-

[1] Webster, W. C., *Recent Centralizing Tendencies in State Educational Administration*, Chap. I.

108

ties. While teacher certification was already a state function in New York in 1900, the rules and regulations have been considerably altered since that time to bring the minimum standards for teachers under the control of the University of the State of New York.

Compulsory attendance laws were first introduced in New York in 1853, in Maryland in 1902, and in North Carolina in 1907. With the increase in staff and power which has come about in the education departments of each of these states, there has been a corresponding increase in their supervision of compulsory attendance.

The length of the school term has been controlled by the central authorities in each of the states studied. North Carolina wrote a provision into her constitution of 1876 making a four months' term mandatory. New York first established a thirty-two weeks' school term in 1911 and afterward increased it to thirty-six weeks by act of the 1917 legislature. Maryland made changes in the length of her required school term in 1904, 1916, and 1922.

It is apparent from the foregoing review of the centralizing tendencies discussed by Webster in 1897 that they have continued to be of importance during the present century so far as the three states included in this study are concerned. However, the decline of the district system has not been very evident in New York, and the only one of the three states studied in which definite textbook control has been centralized has been North Carolina.

Thirty-six years ago Webster made the statement, "The principle of state aid to common school education is firmly established."[2] Judging from the states studied, he was quite correct in his assumption. North Carolina has gone to the extreme of complete state support for an eight months' term; Maryland and New York have continued their provision of state aid with many changes more nearly to provide equality of educational opportunity and support.

"It is important for us to note the bearing of state aid upon state control of education," said Webster. "The one naturally and necessarily led to the other."[3] The evidence gathered from this study indicates that only in the case of North Carolina has any large amount of control accompanied the granting of state

[2] *Op. cit.*, p. 11. [3] *Ibid.*, p. 13.

aid, and since North Carolina has only recently taken this step it is not yet possible to tell how public education will be affected. It is true that control of certain *externa* and *interna* has taken place in each of the three states considered in this study, and that this control has sometimes been enforced by provision for the withholding of state funds for education in the event that the districts within the state refuse to comply with the law, rule, or regulation of the state. However, in Maryland supervision and leadership have functioned in most matters rather than control, and in New York control has largely been applied to minimum requirements rather than to maximum standards.

In the centralizing of educational administration in its school system, the State of North Carolina has gone to the extreme of state control of budgets and finances for a term of eight months. While this extreme centralization has taken place within the state, the financial administration of the school has been centered in a State School Commission which is not under the control of the State Department of Education. This means that the administration of the public schools is divided between two bodies, with the newer and more political one possessing the greater power. Strict accounting for any and all expenditures for public education, with a virtual denial of opportunity for the functioning of local initiative, seems to characterize the present administration of the schools of North Carolina.

In New York State the development of a strong State Education Department has accompanied and promoted the growth of other factors tending toward a centralization of the administration of public education. The judicial power of the Commissioner of Education of New York State has been of vital importance in interpreting and enforcing state laws and regulations concerning education. The movement toward a larger local unit of administration has only resulted in the creation of supervisory districts and a relatively small number of consolidations of local districts. New York has been outstanding for its position in regard to Regents Examinations, licensing of all schools, control of the professions, state aid, and provision for handicapped children. The watchwords of the University of the State of New York seem to be: Maintain minimum standards throughout the state, continue the curriculum-determining Regents Examinations, bring about larger local units of administration by making consolidation profitable to participating districts, and seek further means of securing equality of educational opportunity and support.

The manner in which centralization has been effected has been discussed in the preceding paragraphs and Webster's statements have been compared with the more recent evidence from the three states included in this study. The developments of the past thirty-three years do not appear to have been guided by any one principle or system of distribution of administrative authority between central and local units, despite the fact that each state was trying to achieve a definite result, namely, a good state system of public education. This apparent lack of a guiding principle may be explained in two ways—the legislators voting for some of the acts affecting public education were not sufficiently conversant with education or with previous legislation; the educational administrators in the State Departments of Education either had no long-term program prepared or they were unable to convince the legislators of the need of following such a program.

This study of legislation enacted for schools in three important states shows the development of centralizing tendencies without any evidence of a controlling philosophy of government or of educational administration. A cursory examination of educational legislation in the other states of the Union fails to reveal any greater consistency in their programs of legislation. The issue of central versus local control is one of the most important problems facing those who would develop wisely the legislative program of a state. It seems important, therefore, to conclude this study with a statement of principles which may be used by administrators and legislators in evaluating the proposed legislation which is brought to them for their criticism or approval.

A fundamental reason for the lack of consistency found in the legislative enactments studied is that in most states the local units of administration are not yet large enough to make it reasonably certain that competent local educational officers will be employed. The absence of competent local leadership has usually brought about an insistent demand for legislation to guarantee a minimum of efficiency throughout the state. When this occurs, the division between local control and initiative and central authority disappears. (Present efficiency is considered of more importance than the following of a sound theory of administration. This will probably continue to be true until the reorganization of state educational systems has provided for larger local units of taxation and administration.   These larger units of taxation and administration will make the development of local initiative possible and will enable each unit to carry out intelligently its responsibility for the maintenance of an adequate system of education.   In the following quotation Mort discusses advantages and difficulties in the organization of larger local units:

Another factor related to local initiative is the organization of local tax districts.   No matter how wealthy a district may be, it is not able to exercise local initiative if the area over which it has control is so small that it cannot operate a complete school system.   Districts thus unable to present a desirable educational program must combine in one way or another with other school districts to remedy the situation.   The difficulties involved in these coöperative enterprises are frequently so great as to be real handicaps to the proper development of the educational system.[4]

Granting the necessity for the establishment of local units of administration in which professional leadership is provided, it is possible to distinguish certain principles which should control in the area discussed in this study.   Legislators and educational administrators are vitally concerned with legislation which will differentiate between the functions which should be left to local control and those which should be assumed by the state.   These guiding principles are as follows:

1. The state should guarantee support for local school systems in order to make an acceptable foundation program of education available throughout its entire area.

The report of the National Conference on the Financing of Education discusses the minimum or foundation program as follows:

The principle of equalization reposes a large degree of importance in the minimum program.   It will prove helpful to think of this element in the equalization plan as the *foundation program*.   At any given time of determination it should answer the question as to what constitutes a reasonably satisfactory program in the support of which the state as such shall participate.   This foundation program becomes that part of the total public school program towards which state funds are applied to supplement local levies in effecting the purpose of equalization.   It should be determined through careful research into actual conditions and practice within the state.   The experience of many states shows that this research, although difficult, can be successfully accomplished.

The extent and definition of the foundation program is a matter for each state to decide for itself in the light of actual conditions.   It is most commonly

4 Mort, Paul R., *State Support for Public Education*, p. 187.

to be thought of as the financial measure of that educational offering which will be made available to all children of the state regardless of where they may reside or the financial ability of their district or residence. This educational offering will be provided through state support and a local contribution which is based on uniform effort throughout the state.[5]

2. The state's program for financing schools should be in the nature of a minimum program in order to preserve local initiative and opportunity for experimentation. The localities should be permitted and encouraged to provide at their own expense for a more generous educational program than that paid for by the state.

The report of the National Conference recognizes the importance of local initiative accompanied by strong educational leadership from the central authority:

What seems to be most desired in determining the foundation program within a state is to assure each local school district, through state agencies, a basic amount of money. To be sure, certain standards are also desired. These can be secured in part through basic laws, penalties, and, if necessary, the "earmarking" of parts of the program. But to a very large extent standards come through sound educational leadership. Where state and local educational leadership is not so strong as might be desired, a partial "earmarking" may be justified. Sometimes other conditions warrant types of "earmarking" through formative stages in the reorganization of local units. At the same time it should be remembered that the best route to satisfactory standards and control is through a strong educational leadership which will guide local initiative and safeguard the school program.[6]

Further, as the Report of the National Survey points out, it is possible to break away from the attitude that control must always accompany financial support and that shifting of support must be accompanied by shifting of control. It is possible to distribute funds for the financing of a minimum program and still leave to the local administrative units the determination of the details of this program. To quote from the Report:

Local autonomy has played an important rôle in the financing of public schools. As a result, localities have come to cherish it to such an extent that it has become a complicating element in the whole financial problem. The belief in a correlation between the source of support and the situs of control has been developed by the traditions of our people. It has been one of the main bones of contention in the consideration of Federal support for education. Many state-aid systems have been developed on the assumption that the two are inseparable. It is only within recent years that the possibility of dividing

---

[5] National Conference on the Financing of Education, *Report*, pp. 23–24.   [6] *Ibid.*, p. 25.

the two has been given serious consideration. Even yet the traditional attitude that the two are inseparable springs up to complicate the situation whenever
plans for shifting support to the state are considered.

That progress in thinking along this line has been made, however, is well
illustrated by the fact that this assumption that control and support may be
divided underlies the report of the National Advisory Committee on Education.
The progress of the development of equalization programs based on objective
measures rather than on the administrative judgment of state officials gives
further proof of the willingness of the American people to break away from
the traditional attitude that every dollar which the state provides for schools
should be accompanied by the shifting of commensurate control from the
locality to the state.

One of the outstanding contributions to the clarification of this problem has
been the development of the realization that in the mere construction of taxing
programs the state, as such, does not necessarily become possessed of funds
by virtue of the fact that it acts as a tax-collector.   Present activities looking
toward the use by the state of taxes other than the property tax in order to raise
funds which may be used to relieve the local property tax point to this conclusion.   If the state collects taxes which, because of the difficulty of localizing situs,
cannot be satisfactorily collected by local government and wishes to make the
yield of such taxes available to localities, the degree of control of expenditure
by the state would seem to be a matter of choice, so far as underlying theory
is concerned.   Good policy in any given instance might demand complete control by the state.   On the other hand, it might demand complete freedom on the
part of the local governmental body.   This would seem to be a question to be
settled in each individual instance.   The fact that the state must act as a collecting agency for many new taxes creates an administrative problem of
transferring new funds to the spending agencies in such a way as to replace
the funds now being collected from old taxes.   The element of control necessarily associated with this is therefore limited to the establishment of safe-
guards to prevent the diversion of such funds from the purposes for which they
were collected.   It does not reach into the more basic problem of shifting actual
control over expenditure from local to state officials.

. . . .

In the development of an equalization program on an objective basis the
degree of control is an independent feature to be settled as a separate problem,
once a program of equalization has been devised.   Funds may be granted to a
district in sufficient amounts to finance the minimum program without the
imposition of regulations governing the nature of that program.   In other
words, the state as the sovereign may delegate to local districts the responsibility of determining the exact nature of the minimum program.[7]

3. Control of minimum standards for school sites, buildings,
and equipment should be placed in the State Department of
Education.   No state should permit the location, construction, or

---

[7] Mort, Paul R., *op. cit.*, pp. 149–151.   Report of the National Survey of School Finance.

equipment of its school buildings to fall below definite minimum standards of provision for safety and health and for adequate housing of the educational program.

The state control should not interfere with the desire of any locality to provide schoolhouse construction superior to the minimum standards established. Local initiative and opportunity for experimentation should be maintained even in external matters. This is essential to educational progress.

4. The state should be made responsible for the establishment of standards and for the administration of a system of certification. This certification system should guarantee to all localities competent teachers, supervisors, superintendents, and other professional employees.

Any local unit of administration should be allowed to establish a qualifying system of its own for professional employees, provided the standards are made higher than those embodied in the state system.

5. State control over the curricula and courses of study of the schools should be limited to the enforcement of general requirements considered essential to the safety and perpetuity of the state. Local control should govern the detailed content of courses of study and the selection of the curricula best adapted to the needs of the children.

When any local unit of administration lacks competent professional advice, the state should provide courses of study and curricula.

6. The state should provide leadership in matters relating to the *interna* (especially courses of study, curricula, and methods of teaching) even though the control be left to the local units of administration. This leadership should be under the direction of competent specialists employed by the state and should be provided even when the local administration and supervision within the state are on a high level.

7. The State Department of Education should be given legislative authority in regard to the minimum scope and organization of local school systems. No state should permit the continuance of inadequately organized local school units when this situation can be remedied by reorganization. At the present time local

boards of education are sometimes required by the state to provide night schools, continuation schools, special classes, and the like.

Local authorities should be encouraged to experiment within the general requirements laid down by the state.

8. The State Department of Education should provide leadership in the reorganization of small and inefficient units of administration into units large enough to employ competent administrators and supervisors. It will be the part of wisdom to encourage this local reorganization rather than to try to legislate it. In the preliminary report of a state school survey the gradual abandonment of the small school district is recommended:

The people locally, however, should have the assistance of the highest school officials in the state and in the county in certain matters pertaining to their schools. The combined wisdom of people and of school authorities should be used in the solution of problems that affect many interests through a long period of time.

Gradual abandonment of the small district and its school: From the preceding discussion we have reached the conclusion that we cannot reasonably hope to improve the one-teacher school. The road to progress does not lead that way. There remains but one choice. It is that the small district and its school must eventually be abandoned. It takes some courage seriously to set out on such a course of action. However, these changes do not have to come in one great cataclysmic effort. The fact is that they should come gradually, through development and growth, extending over a period of years. Furthermore, as indicated before, this process of change is not new in the state. It has had a beginning. It needs encouragement to continue.

The recommendations that follow are made to provide a way for the abandonment of small districts. They are grouped into two general parts, viz., *redistricting* and *transportation*. Both should have legislative sanction to become operative.[8]

To quote from the *National Survey of School Finance:*

The problem of amalgamating small, inadequate districts for purposes of increased efficiency is one of the outstanding problems in caring for local initiative. Adequate local organization does not imply a loss of control on the part of the locality; but there is a loss of control as long as the small districts remain, because their powers, hemmed in and hampered, have all but died because of lack of exercise. The reorganization of rural school tax districts, then, is not an attack upon local self-government. On the contrary, it is a desirable step in restoring to the modern citizen a right which earlier generations, faced with simpler educational needs, were able to exercise in the antiquated tax district.[9]

[8] Strayer, George D., Director, *A Preliminary Report of the Survey of the Public Schools of Missouri*, p. 128.   [9] Mort, Paul R., *op. cit.*, p. 188.

9. One general principle should be followed in all legislation dealing with the shifting of control between the state and the locality—the state's control should never be limited to matters of legislative enactment. The State Department of Education should stimulate progress by means of scientific inquiry and through the highest type of professional leadership.

The greatest need at the present time is not for more legislation that will place power and authority in the hands of politically chosen state officials, but for the development of State Departments of Education that are provided with larger and extremely competent staffs, ready and eager to give the highest type of professional service to all the localities within the state. Creative supervision, technical and competent, will bring about local competence and will encourage local initiative.

The greatest educational progress in local communities and in the state is dependent upon freedom to experiment locally in the organization of schools and classes, in the development of courses of study and curricula, in methods of teaching, and in the provision of new services not commonly associated with classroom procedure.

The state should control certain minimum provisions with regard to financial support, qualifications of personnel, school organization, and physical equipment. These state controls aid in the realization of the purpose of the state through public education.

Centralizing tendencies should be encouraged when they attempt to insure adequate financial support, competent personnel, necessary physical equipment, and essential school organization. However, state control over these *externa* should extend only to certain minimum requirements necessary for the operation of a satisfactory minimum program of education. The localities should be encouraged to exceed the state requirements.

The acceptance and utilization of the principles discussed above by administrators and legislators may be expected to bring about a clarification of many of the legislative problems which vex them. Thus, it may also be expected that these principles will contribute to the development of better state programs of education.

BIBLIOGRAPHY

ALEXANDER, UHLMAN S. *Special Legislation Affecting Public Schools*, Chapter II, V, and VII. Contributions to Education, No. 353. New York: Bureau of Publications, Teachers College, Columbia University, 1929. 141 pp.

BETTERS, PAUL V. (editor). "A State System of Schools in North Carolina." *State Centralization in North Carolina*. Institute for Government Research, Studies in Administration, No. 26. Washington, D. C.: Brookings Institution. 261 pp.

BEUMER, E. H. *Centralizing Tendencies in State Educational Administration*. Unpublished Master's Thesis, University of Illinois, 1925. 134 pp.

BRUBACHER, JOHN S. *The Judicial Power of the New York State Commissioner of Education*. Contributions to Education, No. 295. New York: Bureau of Publications, Teachers College, Columbia University, 1927. 173 pp.

BRYCE, JAMES. *Modern Democracies*. Vol. I (second edition). New York: The Macmillan Company, 1924. 508 pp.

COOK, ALBERT S. "Centralizing Tendencies in Educational Administration." *Educational Administration and Supervision*, 4: 133–40, March, 1918.

COOK, ALBERT S. *Equalizing Educational Opportunities in Maryland*. Maryland School Bulletin, XII: No. 1, September, 1930. Baltimore: State Department of Education. 79 pp.

CUBBERLEY, ELLWOOD P. *Public School Administration*. Boston: Houghton Mifflin Company, 1916. 479 pp.

CUBBERLEY, ELLWOOD P. *State School Administration*. Boston: Houghton Mifflin Company, 1927. 773 pp.

FAIRLIE, JOHN A. *The Centralization of Administration in New York State*. Doctor's dissertation. New York: Columbia University, 1898. 210 pp.

FLANDERS, JESSE K. *Legislative Control of the Elementary Curriculum*. Contributions to Education, No. 195. New York: Bureau of Publications, Teachers College, Columbia University, 1925. 242 pp.

GENERAL EDUCATION BOARD. *Public Education in North Carolina*. Raleigh, N. C.: Edwards and Broughton Printing Company, 1920. 137 pp.

HOLCOMBE, ARTHUR N. *State Government in the United States*. (Third edition.) New York: The Macmillan Company, 1931. 703 pp.

KANDEL, I. L. *Comparative Education*. Boston: Houghton Mifflin Company, 1933. 922 pp.

KANDEL, I. L. *Essays in Comparative Education*. Studies of the International Institute, No. 11. New York: Bureau of Publications, Teachers College, Columbia University, 1930. 235 pp.

KNIGHT, EDGAR W. *Public School Education in North Carolina*. Boston: Houghton Mifflin Company, 1916. 384 pp.

LASKI, HAROLD J. *A Grammar of Politics.* New Haven, Conn.: Yale University Press, 1925. 672 pp.

MACIVER, R. M. *The Modern State.* New York: Oxford University Press, 1926. 504 pp.

MARYLAND, STATE OF
By-Laws of the State Board of Education, 1929.
Code of Public General Laws of Maryland, 1888; 1898 Supplement to the 1888 Code.
Maryland Constitution, 1868.
Session Laws, 1872; 1900–1933.

MATZEN, JOHN M. *State Constitutional Provisions for Education.* Contributions to Education, No. 462. New York: Bureau of Publications, Teachers College, Columbia University, 1931. 159 pp.

MORT, PAUL R. *State Support for Public Education.* Report of the National Survey of School Finance. Washington, D. C.: American Council on Education, 1933. 496 pp.

NATIONAL ADVISORY COMMITTEE ON EDUCATION. *Federal Relations to Education.* (In two volumes). Washington, D. C.: National Capitol Press, 1931.

NATIONAL CONFERENCE ON THE FINANCING OF EDUCATION. *Report.* Washington, D. C.: Department of Superintendence, 1933. 78 pp.

NATIONAL EDUCATION ASSOCIATION. "A Self-Survey Plan for State School Systems." *Research Bulletin of the National Education Association,* Vol. 8, No. 2, March, 1930.

NATIONAL EDUCATION ASSOCIATION, RESEARCH DIVISION. *Staffs and Salaries in State Departments of Education.* Studies in State Educational Administration, No. 9. Washington, D. C.: National Education Association, 1931.

NEW YORK, STATE OF
New York State Constitution, 1895.
Session Laws, 1784, 1786, 1812, 1814, 1834, 1848, 1863, 1867, 1877, 1885, 1887, 1889, 1890, 1893, 1895; 1900–1933.

NEW YORK, STATE OF. *Report of the Governor's Committee on the Costs of Public Education in the State of New York,* 1933. 101 pp.

NORTH CAROLINA, STATE OF
North Carolina Constitution, 1876.
North Carolina Reports, Vol. 145, p. 170, 1907.
Supplement to North Carolina Code, 1929.
Session Laws, 1901–1933.

PRESIDENT'S RESEARCH COMMITTEE ON SOCIAL TRENDS. *Report, Recent Social Trends in the United States.* Vol. II, Chap. XXV, "The Growth of Governmental Functions," Leonard D. White; Chap. XXVII, "Public Administration," Carroll H. Wooddy. New York: McGraw-Hill Book Company, Inc., 1933.

RUSSELL, WILLIAM F. "School Administration and Conflicting American Ideals." *Teachers College Record,* XXXI:17–23, October, 1929.

SOPER, WAYNE W. *Development of State Support of Education in New York.* University of the State of New York, Bulletin No. 1019, May, 1933. Albany, University of the State of New York, 1933. 69 pp.

STRAYER, GEORGE D., Director. *A Preliminary Report of the Survey of the Public Schools of Missouri.* Jefferson City, Mo.: State Survey Commission, 1929. 266 pp.

STRAYER, GEORGE D. "The Structure of Government and Its Effect on the Administration of the Schools." *Critical Problems in School Administration,* pp. 7–20. Twelfth Yearbook of the Department of Superintendence. Washington, D. C.: National Education Association, 1934. 383 pp.

STRAYER, GEORGE D. and HAIG, ROBERT M. *The Financing of Education in the State of New York.* The Educational Finance Inquiry, Vol. 1. New York: The Macmillan Company, 1924. 205 pp.

SWIFT, FLETCHER HARPER. *Federal and State Policies in Public School Finance in the United States.* Boston: Ginn and Company, 1931. 472 pp.

TIDWELL, CLYDE J. *State Control of Textbooks.* Contributions to Education, No. 299. New York: Bureau of Publications, Teachers College, Columbia University, 1928. 78 pp.

WEBSTER, WILLIAM C. *Recent Centralizing Tendencies in State Educational Administration.* Doctor's dissertation. New York: Columbia University, 1897. 78 pp.

WHITE, LEONARD D. "Trends in Public Administration." *Recent Social Trends in the United States,* Part I, Chap. VI, XI, and X. New York: McGraw-Hill Book Company, 1933. 365 pp.

INDEX

Academic quota, N. Y., 77, 85, 86
Academy, N. Y., 71, 72
Administration, local unit of, 5, 110, 111, 112, 115, 116; Md., 53, 60, 67; N. Y., 74, 75, 88, 96, 107; N. C., 22, 23, 25, 26
Agriculture, N. Y., 73, 74, 75, 90, 101, 104, 105
Alcoholism, N. C., 36
Allen, A. T., 29
Americanism, N. C., 36
Americanization quota, N. Y., 85
Arbor Day, N. C., 36
Board of Equalization and Review, N. C., 25, 26
Board of Regents, N. Y., 69, 71, 72, 74, 89, 91, 92, 99, 101, 102, 103, 104, 106
Bonded indebtedness, N. Y., 78, 87, 89
Brooks, Supt., N. C., 40
Brubacher, J. S., 97
Bryce, James, 6
Budget, county, N. C., 23, 24, 26; publicity for, N. Y., 83, 88
Building quota, N. Y., 80, 86, 87
Centralization, definition of, 4
Central high school districts, N. Y., 75
Central rural districts, N. Y., 73, 80, 81, 85, 87, 88
Certification of teachers, 5, 108, 109, 115, 117; Division of, 40; Md., 61, 62, 63, 64, 65; N. C., 38, 39, 40
Children, handicapped, 110; Md., 54, 55; N. Y., 78, 82, 84, 85, 95, 102, 105, 106; mentally retarded, N. Y., 84, 85, 102; physically defective, N. Y., 75, 79, 82, 85, 102, 105
Citizenship, and patriotism, N. Y., 103, 104, 106
Cole Law, N. Y., 81, 83
Colored industrial schools, Md., 51, 52
Commissioner of Education, N. Y., 72, 74, 75, 76, 77, 79, 80, 82, 89, 90, 91, 92, 96, 98, 103, 104, 105, 106, 107
Commissioner's judicial power, N. Y., 96, 110

Community civics, Md., 59
Compulsory attendance, 5, 108, 109; Md., 54, 64, 65; N. C., 26
Consolidated districts, N. Y., 79, 85, 87, 88, 93, 97, 98, 107, 110
Constitution, Md., 49, 59; N. Y., 68; N. C., 17, 36; United States, 36, 59, 104, 106
Continuation schools, N. Y., 73, 86, 104, 115
County budget, N. C., 23, 24, 26
County Government Advisory Commission, N. C., 24
County superintendent of schools, N. C., 43
Courses of study, 5, 108, 115, 117; Md., 58; N. Y., 76, 89, 101, 103; N. C. 34
Cubberley, Ellwood P., 4, 6
Distribution of funds, 19, 20
District quota, N. Y., 70, 71, 73, 85, 87
District superintendent, N. Y., 82, 90, 93, 94
District system, 5, 108, 109
Districts, central high school, N. Y., 75; central rural, N. Y., 73, 80, 81, 85, 87, 88; consolidated, N. Y., 79, 85, 87, 88, 93, 97, 98, 107, 110; one-teacher, N. Y., 82, 84; school hygiene, N. Y., 79; special tax, N. C., 28.
Division, of Negro Education, N. C., 41; of Schoolhouse Planning, N. C., 32, 33; of Teacher Training, N. C., 41
Educational Finance Inquiry, 9, 10
Equality of opportunity, 5, 9, 10, 109, 111, 112; Md., 55, 58, 60, 66; N. Y., 88, 94, 96, 97, 100, 106, 107; N. C. 20, 33, 38, 44, 46
Equalization, quota, N. Y., 81, 83, 87; Plan of, Md., 52, 53; State Board of, N. C., 24, 25, 42, 46
Expenditures, N. Y., 75, 80, 81, 83, 84; publicity for, 83, 88
Externa, 11–14, 110, 117; Md., 56, 58, 66; N. Y., 88, 94, 98; N. C., 29, 34, 38, 45, 46, 47
Fairlie, J. A. 3, 68
Farm schools, N. Y., 74, 101
Fire prevention, N. Y., 104, 106